ethical
ce
ournal
Ethics

Aims and scope

The commitment of the academic quarterly, *Ethical Space*, is to examine significant historical and emerging ethical issues in communication. Its guiding principles are:

- internationalism,
- independent integrity,
- respect for difference and diversity,
- interdisciplinarity,
- theoretical rigour,
- practitioner focus.

In an editorial in Vol. 3, Nos 2 and 3 of 2006, the joint editor, Donald Matheson, of Canterbury University, New Zealand, stresses that ethics can be defined narrowly, as a matter of duty or responsibility, or ethics can be defined broadly 'blurring into areas such as politics and social criticism'. *Ethical Space* stands essentially at the blurred end of the definitional range. Dr Matheson observes: 'As many commentators have pointed out, a discussion of ethics that is divorced from politics is immediately unable to talk about some of the most important factors in shaping communication and media practices.'

The journal, then, aims to provide a meeting point for media experts, scholars and practitioners who come from different disciplines. Moreover, one of its major strands is to problematise professionalism (for instance, by focusing on alternative, progressive media) and highlight many of its underlying myths.

Submissions

Papers should be submitted to the Editor via email. Full details on submission – along with detailed notes for authors – are available online:
www.ethical-space.co.uk

www.ethical-space.co.uk

Subscription Information

Each volume contains 4 issues, issued quarterly. Enquiries regarding subscriptions and orders, both in the UK and overseas, should be sent to:

Journals Fulfilment Department
Abramis Academic
ASK House
Northgate Avenue
Bury St. Edmunds
Suffolk
IP32 6BB
UK

Tel: +44 (0)1284 717884   Email: info@abramis.co.uk

Your usual subscription agency will also be able to take a subscription to *Ethical Space*.

For the current annual subscription costs please see the subscription information page at the back of this issue.

Publishing Office
Abramis Academic
ASK House
Northgate Avenue
Bury St. Edmunds
Suffolk
IP32 6BB
UK

Tel: +44 (0)1284 717884
Fax: +44 (0)1284 717889
Email: info@abramis.co.uk
Web: www.abramis.co.uk

Copyright
All rights reserved. No part of this publication may be reproduced in any material form (including photocopying or storing it in any medium by electronic means, and whether or not transiently or incidentally to some other use of this publication) without the written permission of the copyright owner, except in accordance with the provisions of the Copyright, Designs and Patents Act 1988, or under terms of a licence issued by the Copyright Licensing Agency Ltd, 33-34, Alfred Place, London WC1E 7DP, UK. Applications for the copyright owner's permission to reproduce part of this publication should be addressed to the Publishers.

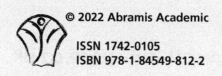

© 2022 Abramis Academic

ISSN 1742-0105
ISBN 978-1-84549-812-2

ethical
space

The International Journal
of Communication Ethics

Contents

Copyright 2023-1. Ethical Space: The International Journal of Communication Ethics. All rights reserved. Vol 20, No 1 2023   **1**

Editorial Board

Joint Editors

Donald Matheson	University of Canterbury, New Zealand
Sue Joseph	University of South Australia
Tom Bradshaw	University of Gloucestershire

Emeritus Editor

Richard Lance Keeble	University of Lincoln

Reviews Editors

Sue Joseph	University of South Australia
David Baines	Newcastle University

Editorial board members

Raphael Alvira	University of Navarra
Mona Baker	Manchester University
Jay Black	Founding editor, Journal of Mass Media Ethics
Antonio Castillo	RMIT University, Melbourne
Saviour Chircop	University of Malta
Clifford Christians	University of Illinois-Urbana, USA
Raphael Cohen–Almagor	University of Hull
Tom Cooper	Emerson College, Boston, MA
Roger Domeneghetti	Northumbria University
Deni Elliott	University of Montana
Chris Frost	Liverpool John Moores University
Theodore L. Glasser	Stanford University
Paul Jackson	Manchester Business School
Mike Jempson	Hon. Director, MediaWise Trust
Cheris Kramarae	University of Oregon; Centre for the Study of Women in Society
John Mair	Book editor
Ian Mayes	Former *Guardian* Readers' Editor
Jolyon Mitchell	University of Edinburgh
Colleen Murrell	Dublin City University
Kaarle Nordenstreng	Tampere University
Manuel Parez i Maicas	Universitat Autonoma de Barcelona
Julian Petley	Brunel University
Ian Richards	University of South Australia, Adelaide
Simon Rogerson	De Montfort University
Lorna Roth	Concordia University, Montreal
Karen Sanders	St Mary's University
John Steel	Sheffield University
Ben Stubbs	University of South Australia
Miklos Sukosd	University of Copenhagen
Barbara Thomass	Ruhruniversität Bochum
Terry Threadgold	Centre for Journalism Studies, Cardiff University
Stephen J. Ward	University of British Columbia
James Winter	University of Windsor, Canada

Richard Lance Keeble,
University of Lincoln

ES: A journal committed to reflection and promoting ethical action

This year, *Ethical Space* celebrates its twentieth anniversary. Yes: we have come through! In the journal's first editorial, in early 2003, I wrote: 'Ethics is about reflection (cultivating the ethical space) and action. *ES* … is certainly committed to inspiring rigorous and lively reflection of international communication issues and ultimately to promoting ethical action. Why not join the debate?'

Today many communication professionals, activists and academics are taking action in support of Julian Assange, the WikiLeaks founder, still held in Belmarsh high security prison in London (normally reserved for terrorists and members of organised crime gangs) on trumped-up charges of treason for exposing US war crimes in Iraq and Afghanistan. Such ethical action in backing Assange is crucial in protecting press freedom and free expression.

On 17 July, the UK home secretary, Priti Patel, signed off an order for Assange's extradition to the US where he is wanted by authorities on 18 counts, including a spying charge, relating to WikiLeaks's release of vast troves of confidential US military records and diplomatic cables which Washington says put lives in danger. If found guilty, Assange faces 175 years in a maximum security jail. The prosecution of Assange is based on the 1917 Espionage Act which has never been used before to prosecute either a publisher or broadcaster.

Assange's defence team immediately announced they would challenge the extradition order in the High Court. Moreover, some 600,000 journalists represented by the International Federation of Journalists and its 147 member unions, plus press freedom advocates, like PEN, Reporters Without Borders, the National Lawyers Guild, the Center for Investigative Journalism, FAIR and many more have demanded freedom for Julian Assange.

Richard Lance Keeble

In November 2022, ten years after Assange was forced to seek refuge at the Ecuadorian embassy in London and three years after he was arrested and subjected to solitary confinement, the editors and publishers of *The New York Times*, the *Guardian*, *Le Monde*, *El País* and *Der Spiegel* issued an open letter calling on US President Joe Biden to end Assange's prosecution. They say: 'Obtaining and disclosing sensitive information when necessary in the public interest is a core part of the daily work of journalists. If that work is criminalised, our public discourse and our democracies are made significantly weaker.' On 28 November 2010, the same five newspapers had published in cooperation with WikiLeaks what became know as 'Cable gate', a set of 251,000 confidential cables from the US State Department which revealed corruption, diplomatic scandals and spy affairs on an international scale.

But as Thomas Scripps writes: 'At long last, these publications have acknowledged that the material published by Assange was of vital public interest and importance. ... But this raises the question: What took so long? Why did it take 10 years for *The New York Times* and *Guardian* to call for Assange's prosecution to end?'[1]

Australian Labor prime minister Anthony Albanese also ended months of silence on the issue in November saying his government had called on President Biden to end the 'legal action' against his fellow countryman Assange. A similar appeal was made by Adele Ferguson, chair of the Walkley Foundation in Australia.

Katherine Gun, the whistleblower who revealed the UK's attempts to influence the UN vote in favour of the Iraq invasion of 2003, commented:

> In my opinion, mainstream journalists failed to see or at any rate report on how it could impact on journalism and publishing until quite recently. I suspect that due to the lack of a strong and united resistance encompassing the UK press and broadcasting journalists, the government has been emboldened to raise the possibility of altering the Official Secrets Act, further eroding press freedom and freedom of speech, potentially equating unauthorised disclosures with espionage for whistleblowers as well as journalists.[2]

The role of WikiLeaks in publishing the revelations of whistleblowers (protected by its encryption system), exposing the lies and corruption of governments, banks, political parties, war planners and the corporate media, has been documented in an article on the *News International* website[3] by Felicity Ruby, a doctoral candidate in the Department of Government and International Relations at the University of Sydney, and Naomi Colvin, of the international NGO Blueprint for Free Speech:

- Cables revealed the UK's establishment of a marine reserve around Diego Garcia to protect the US base and prevent the Chagos Islanders from ever returning home.

- The International Atomic Energy Authority had warned Japan on safety issues at nuclear plants in 2009, years before the Fukushima disaster, particularly that its power plants could not withstand powerful earthquakes.

- Australia worked with Britain, Canada, Japan and others to undermine the cluster munitions treaty, ensuring that deploying US cluster bombs on their soil was not precluded by the convention.

- Safety and security issues with the UK's Trident nuclear weapons system were revealed to WikiLeaks by Royal Navy Able Seaman William McNeilly.

- The Minton Report detailed how Dutch multinational company Trafigura had dumped toxic waste in Ivory Coast, so threatening 108,000 people. WikiLeaks published the report that had been suppressed through a super injunction.

- The Obama administration spied on UN leadership and personnel, authorising the theft of biometric data (DNA, fingerprints, retina scans) and passwords.

- El-Masri, a completely innocent German citizen, snatched off the streets, detained, tortured and dumped on a street in Albania, used six cables in evidence when he took a case to the European Court of Human Rights.

- The Syria Files exposed the workings of the Assad regime through over two million emails from 680 Syrian political figures, ministries and associated companies and the regime's international security contracts.

- The Guantanamo Files exposed routine violations of the Geneva Conventions and abuse of 800 prisoners as young as fourteen and as old as eighty-nine at Guantanamo Bay.

- The Collateral Murder classified US military video, revealed by Chelsea Manning, showed a helicopter gunship killing eighteen people in Baghdad, including two Reuters journalists and their rescuers, thus documenting a war crime. In 2013, Manning was jailed for 35 years for exposing war crimes, though she was released in 2017 after President Obama commuted her sentence.

- The United States created a manual for unconventional warfare in 2008 for US Special Forces when they are overthrowing a government. The media's role in advancing the goals of US national power is highlighted in the manual.

- US forces were responsible for the death and maiming of more than 200,000 people in Iraq.

- The Global Intelligence Files revealed the activities of private intelligence firm Stratfor, which services the US government and large corporations such as Bhopal's Dow Chemical Company, Lockheed Martin, Raytheon and numerous government agencies.

Richard Lance
Keeble

- The National Security Agency (NSA) intercepted communication of targets, including UN secretary-general Ban Ki-Moon's meetings with heads of state, Prime Ministers Berlusconi and Netanyahu, President Hollande, the Japanese cabinet, the UNHCR and the World Trade Organisation.

- In 2016, a corrupt multibillion-dollar conflict was fuelled by Western and Chinese companies which grabbed uranium and other mining rights in the Central African Republic (CAR) and escaped paying for the environmental consequences.

- Cash payments were made to Indian MPs for their support of a US-India nuclear deal.

- Myanmar shipped 10,000 tons of rice to feed poor North Korea as payment for sophisticated conventional weapons. The cable refers to a business source stating that exchanges of weapons for food had gone on for more than five years.

- See *Secret Power: WikiLeaks and its Enemies*, by Stefania Maurizi, London: Pluto Press, 2022; https://www.plutobooks.com/9780745347615/secret-power/

Alternative – but with impact

While the mainstream media has failed dismally to acknowledge the implications of the Assange prosecution for press freedom, many alternative media, in contrast, have highlighted his plight and the many campaigns in his defence. A selection of websites and blogs from the UK, America, France, India and Australia includes: amnesty.org; antiwar.com; antonylowenstein.com; assangedefense.org; assangecampaign.org.au; blueprintforfreespeech.net; caitlinjohnstone.com; chomsky.info; coldtype.net; commondreams.org; consortiumnews.com; countercurrents.org; counterfire.org; counterpunch.org; covertactionmagazine.com; craigmurray.org.uk; chrishedges.substack.com (subscription service); declassifieduk.org; declassifiedaus.org; democracynow.org; dissidentvoice.org; dontextraditeassange.com; fpif.org (Foreign Policy in Focus); frontline.thehindu.com; globalresearch.ca (in particular the reporting of Pepe Escobar, Michel Chossudovsky and Scott Ritter); greenleft.org.au; greenwald.substack.com (subscription service); indexoncensorship.org; johnpilger.com; jonathan-cook.net; juancole.com; leftfootforward.org; laprogressive.com; markcurtis.info; middleeasteye.net; mintpressnews.com; mondediplo.com; morningstaronline.co.uk; mronline.org; newint.org; newleftreview.org (in particular the commentaries of Tariq Ali); newmatilda.com; nuj.org.uk; oliverboydbarrett.substack.com (subscription service): paulcraigroberts.org; peacenews.info; popularresistance.org; pressenza.com; progressive.international; rollingstone.com (in particular, the reporting of Matt Taibi); socialistworker.co.uk; thealtworld.com; thegrayzone.com; wiseupaction.info; wsws.org.

You may consider these websites have tiny readerships, are preaching to the converted – and have little impact. You would be wrong. Take just the example of declassifieduk.org. An investigative report by Mark Curtis and Matt Kennard, in March 2021, that the British ambassador, Jeff Glekin, played a personal role in the events leading up to the 2019 military-backed coup which removed Bolivia's democratically elected President, Evo Morales, had a major impact in the country. The foreign minister, Rogelio Mayta, called in the UK ambassador to explain the contents of the article and to report on its findings. An article by Matt Kennard about Argentina's negotiator 'being pissed' when he signed a widely criticised deal with Britain in 2016 led the foreign minister to ordering an investigation into the Declassified report and it was front page news in the country for a week. And it sparked anti-government protests across the country. Phil Miller's reports about Nigerian air force pilots being secretly trained in the UK (followed up by a story about civilians being killed, a marketplace destroyed and a school hit in indiscriminate air strikes) led to the closure of a military helicopter academy in Cornwall linked to human rights abuses. Following another of Miller's investigations, the political opposition in Uganda called for Britain's minister for Africa to resign over his business ties to the Museveni regime.

Moreover, the website has been covering important issues ignored by the mainstream. For instance, it has highlighted the UK's role in the Yemen war, the legal conflicts of interest in the persecution of Julian Assange, the UK's involvement in the 1984 Golden Temple massacre in India, the role played by the British American Project in the UK, Britain's support for Jair Bolsonaro in Brazil and the Oman dictatorship's UK property empire. And reporters Mark Curtis and John McEvoy have exposed the UK's role in the Vietnam War, how Shell and BP helped finance British propaganda, Britain's covert role in the on-going Yemen war, its colonial war in Malaya, its support for Iran's Shah and Margaret Thatcher's support for the US invasion of Panama in 1989.

There is also an excellent Australian edition (at declassifiedaus.org) which has also been publishing important exclusive revelations – for instance, about an anti-Russian 'bot army' pushing disinformation about the Ukraine conflict and how an Australian company secured vast swathes of Afghanistan for mineral and mine exploration in the dying months of the US-backed government.

Press freedom threatened around the world

Assange's indictment comes at a time when press freedom is being threatened around the world. And many of those courageous, committed journalists and media workers who face imprisonment, torture and even death simply for doing their job do not gain the publicity they deserve. In December 2022, the Haitian radio journalist, Francklin Tamar, was shot and killed. In the same month, three television crews were attacked while covering protests in northern

Richard Lance
Keeble

Kosovo. Those involved included camera operator Agon Bejtullahu and driver Elsad Sinan. In Afghanistan, Taliban intelligence officials beat and interrogated brutally journalist Zabihullah Noori.

The annual prison census of the Committee to Protect Journalists found that 363 reporters were deprived of their freedom as of 1 December 2022 – a new global high, beating the previous year's record by 20 per cent. As the CPJ commented: 'It marks another grim milestone in a deteriorating media landscape.' Authoritarian governments were increasingly stifling the media in their attempts to keep the lid on boiling discontent in a world disrupted by Covid-19 and the economic fallout from the conflict in the Ukraine.

The year's top five jailers of journalists were Iran, China, Myanmar, Turkey and Belarus, respectively.[4]

In a new threat to press freedom, the UK government is planning changes to the Official Secrets Act which effectively conflate investigative journalism with spying.[5]

Celebrating 20 years of publication

We have a series of bumper issues planned for our 20th anniversary year. The coverage of indigenous issues is to be the subject of a guest-edited double issue while the final issue of the year is to be guest edited by Tess Scholfield-Peters and focus on Third Generation Holocaust writing.

In addition, we are bringing out two books drawing on papers and articles published by *ES* over the last two decades. Titled ES – *Journal with a difference: Celebrating 20 years*, the first volume will carry papers under the themes of 'Communication ethics: Philosophical reflections', 'New media: New ethical challenges', 'Professionalisation and media ethics: Behind the rhetoric', 'Communication ethics and pedagogy', 'And finally: Speaking out on ethics'. The second volume, appearing later in 2023, will cover 'Directing a critical spotlight on the mainstream', 'Alternative voices', 'Public relations: Beyond propaganda', 'And finally: Speaking out on ethics'.

So more academically rigorous, challenging, original writing – inspiring ethical reflection and action – to look forward to.

Notes

[1] https://www.wsws.org/en/articles/2022/11/29/pers-n29.html

[2] https://propagandainfocus.com/katharine-gun-on-julian-assange/

[3] https://newint.org/features/2019/10/31/journalists-must-pay-attention-julian-assange

[4] https://cpj.org/

[5] https://legaljournal.com/the-official-secrets-act-proposed-reforms-threaten-the-future-of-journalism/

8   Copyright 2022-1. Ethical Space: The International Journal of Communication Ethics. All rights reserved. Vol 20, No 1 2023

Anna Denejkina
Sue Joseph

Collaborative reflection and trauma: Narrative writing as a healing intervention

Narrative writing as a healing intervention involves the repeated recounting of a traumatic event. Research shows the benefits of narrative writing as an intervention for post-traumatic stress and the development of post-traumatic growth. Studies report significant upturn in mood and increase of post-traumatic growth in participants, and less negative emotions related to the recall of the traumatic event. Through the process of collaborative reflection, this paper analyses if the positive effect of narrative writing as intervention for post-traumatic stress is experienced without a structured approach to the activity overseen by a mental health practitioner, and considers the ethics of this process of writing. This paper approaches narrative writing from the medical and humanities models, to illustrate the benefits of an interdisciplinary conversation and approach to narrative writing as intervention for post-traumatic stress.

Key words: post-traumatic stress, collaborative reflection, narrative writing, narrative exposure therapy, autoethnography, doctoral studies

Introduction

> 'Many people, perhaps most, are able to guide their own therapy. Writing itself is a powerful therapeutic technique'
> (Esterling et al. 1999: 94).

Writing about traumatic experiences and events results in benefits to the individual through a mechanism of restructuring autobiographic memory. As Steinberg writes:

> Words are monumental. They contain, record and represent packets of information that commemorate the experiences and

Anna Denejkina

Sue Joseph

relationships, often emotionally loaded and traumatic, in which they were first forged; words contain aeons of human and perhaps pre-human experience in them and in their implications and resonances (Steinberg 2004: 45).

Research suggests that exposure to trauma forms 'multiple fear networks dominated by sensory-perceptual information and [lacks] autobiographical information' (Lely 2019; see also Schauer et al. 2011). By connecting implicit memories of the traumatic event(s) with episodic context and promoting a habituation to these traumatic memories through narrative writing, it is proposed that the individual's memory is reconstructed (Schauer et al. 2011; Phoenix Australia 2020).

For this paper, we are adapting Wright and Chung's definition of writing therapy to define narrative writing therapy as individual 'expressive and reflective writing, whether self-generated or suggested by a therapist/ researcher' (2001: 279).

Through the process of collaborative reflection, this paper examines the positive effect of narrative writing for post-traumatic stress without being overseen by a therapist or lay-therapist, and considers the ethics of this process of writing. It approaches narrative writing from the medical and humanities models to illustrate the benefits of an interdisciplinary research.

Humanities model for trauma narrative writing

> ... trauma happens to us, our friends, our families, and our neighbours ... trauma affects not only those who are directly exposed to it, but also those around them (van der Kolk 2014: 1).

This paper is concerned with not just the re-representation of trauma narrative in creative doctoral studies – without a trauma-informed pedagogy, this is an ethically fraught space – but the reflection upon it, and the effect this can have on the candidate writing into this implicitly deeply private and painful component of a life story. Judith Harris tells us:

> Freud and his theoretical descendants, even those who have challenged his theories, agree that expression, and its opposite, repression operate as powerful invisible agents in human psychic health. The therapeutic effects of writing are as absorbing as they are beneficial (2003: 669).

But doctoral supervisors are not trained in psychotherapy nor even counselling, and institutions historically are neither equipped to deal with supporting supervisors and candidates nor with the potential fall-out from writing trauma narrative as a degree component. Supervisors also are at risk of a level of vicarious trauma through witnessing. Much of the literature around writing as therapy reveals it as curative but this is mostly in a clinical setting. Candidates arriving to the tertiary sector with a conscious or subconscious intent to undertake a life writing, autobiographical or autoethnographic thread underpinned with trauma narrative, render themselves vulnerable to re-traumatisation. As two decades ago, Caruth wrote: 'The story of trauma, then, as the narrative of belated experience, far from telling of an escape from reality … rather attests to its endless impact on a life' (1996: 7). How the narrativising of this is managed by the doctoral supervisor and candidate directly impacts on the candidate's health and well-being, and success of their doctoral undertaking; additionally, as mentioned above, as witness, the supervisor is also at risk of a level of vicarious trauma.

Kearney writes of the healing powers of story-telling as 'knowledge' since the days of Aristotle and the Ancient Greeks. He writes: 'One of the most enduring ethical functions of narrative is catharsis' (2008: 181). Catharsis derives from the Greek *kathairein*, meaning to cleanse or purge. Harking back to Aristotle and his *Poetics* (C. 335 BC), this purging is often of 'pity and fear' through art, bringing with it 'spiritual renewal or release from tension' (*Merriam-Webster* n.d.). Additionally, as Phillips and Rolfe tell us: 'There has been a long Western tradition, originating with Augustine's *Confessions*, of confessional, self-reflective writing that links writing with … well-being' (2016: 193). And as Pascoe writes: 'Although writing has been incorporated into psychotherapy for many years, the effects of writing on physical and mental health have only been empirically studied in the last several decades through the development of expressive writing' (2016: 5).

Accordingly, in 1986 James Pennebaker wrote about the efficacy of narrative writing as a form of remediation for trauma sufferers. He is still writing on this subject, building on his earlier findings along with other scholars in interdisciplinary fields. He argues: 'Converting emotions and images into words changes the way a person organises and thinks about trauma…' He explains: 'By integrating thoughts and feelings … the person can more easily construct a coherent narrative of the process' (2000: 8). Jill Littrell believes that health benefits from the writing of traumatic memory are derived only when an 'inspiring perspective' is found by the individual (2009: 308). She argues:

> If a person revisits painful emotion and is able to construct some new meaning in the experience or to develop some new physiological response to the emotionally evocative material, then the procedure can result in better health and less psychological stress (2009: 306).

Littrell extends her argument by stating that without reappraisal, this rendering is potentially damaging: 'Expression of distress is useful when accompanied by reappraisal but harmful when a new response is not achieved' (2009: 312). Lengelle and Meijers agree: 'The aim of therapeutic writing is to work toward a more life-giving perspective … as a "second story". This may include a shift in perspective, acceptance, or meaning found/constructed' (2009: 59).

Anna Denejkina

Sue Joseph

Yet therapeutic writing is not without its ethical minefields. Care and support must be given at all stages of the writing for both supervisor and candidate. The supervisor has a duty of care to watch and listen, taking cues of distress as red flags for suggested action. If managed well, there is some hope of post-traumatic growth, another method of appraising Littrell's 'inspiring perspective' or re-evaluation. A mid-1990s foundational text, written by Tedeschi and Calhoun, lists a variety of shifting positive outcomes from a traumatic incident. They write: 'At least three broad categories of perceived benefits have been identified: changes in self-perception, changes in interpersonal relationships, and a changed philosophy of life' (Tedeschi and Calhoun 1996: 456). In a later paper drawing on further empirical data, they write: '... the frightening and confusing aftermath of trauma, where fundamental assumptions are severely challenged, can be fertile ground for unexpected outcomes that can be observed in survivors: post-traumatic growth' (2004: 1). Citing their own definition – 'positive psychological change experienced as a result of the struggle with highly challenging life circumstances' (ibid: 1) – they set about developing a framework for how post-traumatic growth happens. They claim that there is nothing new about the notion of post-traumatic growth: 'The general understanding that suffering and distress can be possible sources of positive change is thousands of years old' (ibid: 2) but that it was not until the 1980s and 1990s that scholars looked at these ideas systematically, focusing specifically on 'the possibility of growth from the struggle with trauma' (ibid: 3). As Bolton writes:

> Writing is different from talking; it has a power all of its own. ... It can allow an exploration of cognitive, emotional and spiritual areas otherwise not accessible, and an expression of elements otherwise inexpressible. The very act of creativity – of making something on the page which wasn't there before – tends to increase self-confidence, feelings of self-worth and motivation for life (Bolton 2004: 1).

This notion underpins an ethical view of the commodification of trauma narrative within the tertiary sector and its attendant complexities.

Medical model for trauma narrative writing

Developed in the 1980s by Michael White and David Epston (1990), narrative therapy regards individuals as experts in their own lives through a 'collaborative and non-pathologizing approach to counselling and community work' (Bjoro et al. 2016: 332). Narrative therapy approaches are cooperative and egalitarian between the individual and therapist or counsellor (Payne 2006), developed with recognition of the impact of an individual's position in relation to cultural, social and political contexts (O'Hanlon 1994).

Based within the cognitive behavioural framework, narrative exposure therapy (NET) is a standardised, evidence-based and short-term treatment. NET is used for individuals who have PTSD symptoms resulting from complex trauma histories (Robjant and Fazel 2010), including traumatic events like war, natural disaster and torture (Gwozdziewycz and Mehl-Madrona 2013), as well as substance abuse (Singer et al. 2013). Developed to treat survivors and to document human rights violations, NET is a treatment in which the individual narrates a chronological account of their life story, with a focus on traumatic experiences (Schauer et al. 2005: 199). The narration recounted by the individual is then written up by their therapist between sessions. NET works by 'promoting habituation to traumatic memories through exposure, and reconstructing the individual's autobiographic memory' (Phoenix Australia 2020: 5). NET can be applied on a large scale with research showing its cross-cultural application and efficacy in Western and non-Western countries (Jacob et al. 2014; Stenmark et al. 2013; Lange-Nielsen et al. 2012). NET is a manualised approach (that is performed according to specific guidelines) and can be delivered by non-mental health professionals, with research showing that mental health professionals and non-mental health professionals trained to deliver NET have equivalent efficacy outcomes (Neuner et al. 2008).

Several narrative therapy approaches are used in the treatment of post-traumatic stress disorder (PTSD), including structured writing therapy (Van Emmerik et al. 2008), written exposure therapy (Sloan et al. 2012), narrative exposure therapy for children (KidNET) (Neuner et al. 2008), 'interapy' (Lange et al. 2000) and narrative writing (Sloan et al. 2015). Narrative writing as treatment for PTSD involves the individual 'repeatedly recounting a traumatic event that they have experienced' (ibid: 215), with research showing that this treatment approach to PTSD has a comparable effect to some cognitive behavioural therapies including prolonged exposure therapy (PET) and cognitive processing therapy (CPT) (Benish et al. 2008; also see Hoge 2011). Studies in narrative writing approaches to therapy report:

- improvements in mood and increase of post-traumatic growth in participants and less negative emotions related to the recall of the traumatic event (measured by changes in cortisol) (Smyth et al. 2008);

- reduction in PTS symptom severity (Hirai et al. 2020);

- positive trends toward improving outcomes for individuals with disordered eating (Ramsey-Wade et al. 2020);

- military service members reporting relief and mostly positive emotions during and post-writing intervention (Bronwen et al. 2019);

- and 'improvement in PTSD, depression, moral injury, dissociation and adult attachment reduction' in a cohort of military service members and veterans undertaking an intensive treatment programme incorporating narrative writing (among a treatment protocol of eye movement desensitisation and reprocessing therapy, equine-assisted psychotherapy and yoga) to address the effects of combat trauma in military service members and veterans (Steele et al. 2018).

Anna Denejkina

Sue Joseph

Materials and methods

Collaborative reflection builds on the method of collaborative witnessing, a form of relational autoethnography that helps the researcher to 'focus on and evocatively tell the lives of others in shared storytelling and conversation' (Ellis and Rawicki 2013: 366). Autoethnography is defined as 'an approach to research and writing that seeks to describe and systematically analyze (graphy) personal experience (auto) in order to understand cultural experience (ethno)' (Ellis et al. 2011), with two main domains of autoethnography being evocative autoethnography (Ellis and Bochner 2000) and analytic autoethnography (Haynes 2000). Collaborative witnessing 'extends an autoethnographic perspective in its emphasis on writing for and with the other ... bearing witness to others as well as to oneself' (Ellis and Rawicki 2013: 336).

Collaborative reflection is a process of autoethnographic enquiry in which the authors reflect on previous experience of, in this case, narrative writing about trauma, through a discussion of its experience, processes, benefits and disadvantages, and use reflexivity to consider future application of narrative writing as trauma intervention outside of a manualised or structured approach. This process focused on two written works by the authors, completed prior to the study and interview conducted for this study.

Two trauma narrative works focusing on traumatic experiences written by the authors were selected for this study, *Black tulip* (Denejkina 2019) and *Home* (Joseph 2013). Both of these works are autoethnographic, with the second work using an exo-autoethnographic methodology in the research and writing of the narrative (see Denejkina 2017).

The interview between the two authors was conducted on 19 August 2020 via Zoom: For transparency, Associate Professor Sue Joseph was Dr Anna Denejkina's principal PhD supervisor; today the two researchers are colleagues and research collaborators. The audio was transcribed by a third-party.

Qualitative data was analysed thematically (Braun and Clarke 2012) in three stages: first, the data was individually analysed by both authors; second, both authors reconvened for inter-rater checks of each other's initial analyses; third, authors discussed the thematic analyses and finalised themes produced from the qualitative data.

Results

Results from this study reveal three main findings in relation to the use of trauma narrative writing for healing purposes. Firstly, data suggests that narrative exposure therapy outside manualised (and/or clinical) setting has potential risk; secondly, we found that trauma narratives are not necessarily nor quintessentially therapeutic for individuals who enter them without therapeutic framework. And finally, data suggests that trauma narrative writing outside of the therapeutic framework can be used as a way to recover or regain the *agency* of the writer.

These results are based on five main themes identified in the qualitative data analysis:

1. complex trauma/embodied trauma;
2. divergent from narrative therapy;
3. trauma narrative affect;
4. agency and transparency, and
5. process of uncovering content for writing.

Each theme is detailed below with excerpts provided from the interview transcript to explain the themes. The discussion to follow synthesises the themes with results from the study.

Theme 1: Complex trauma/embodied trauma

Complex trauma is the exposure of an individual to multiple traumatic events, which can vary in nature but have a cumulative effect on the individual (Courtois 2004). Embodied trauma speaks to individuals who go through traumatic experiences and often develop somatic symptoms connected to deep psychological issues resulting from the trauma. Such trauma is embodied in the sub-symbolic mode (an intuitive or implicit process), which involves the affective, somatic, sensory and motor modes of mental processing (Caizzi 2012; Perrella et al. 2016).

The themes of complex and embodied trauma were identified in the interview transcript between the two authors through their descriptions and discussion around the impact of their individual traumatic experiences. These traumatic experiences were narrativised within their respective works. Throughout the interview, the authors' reflections on the traumatic experiences showed their complex trauma and embodied trauma, though the authors did not directly or explicitly speak to either of the topics of complex or embodied trauma in their interviews.

The quotations below show the author of *Home* reflecting on how their traumatic experiences and resultant complex trauma is embodied, describing that for them these experiences are not separate from other facets of their life and that they continue to be present within their unconscious.

> I think I've had trauma swirling around me since I was born. So I haven't separated it from any other event in my life; it just seems to be a part of the fabric of my life. ... But the writing that I've done has always been really organic: I've never planned to write about trauma, it's just happened on a day, or in a week, or at a time (19 August 2020, transcript).

> So running up to when I wrote *Home*, I was going to work on a scholarly paper about place, space and home, and then – absolutely this is no word of a lie – I woke up, it was a Friday morning (I think I had been writing something in my sleep for weeks, without being

Anna Denejkina

Sue Joseph

aware of it), I sat down at the computer with no thought that I was writing anything, not even writing about the space, place, home bit, and I just wrote this [traumatic narrative] (19 August 2020, transcript).

Theme 2: Divergent from narrative therapy

The second theme identified within the transcript speaks to the possible issues with narrative writing as healing intervention when it is undertaken in absence of a therapeutic framework in place for the writer, such as without a structured or manualised approach to the activity overseen by a therapist or lay-therapist. The emergence of this theme counters the ideas presented through the humanities model presented earlier in this article that trauma narratives are healing, with some writing in this domain suggesting, or can be interpreted as, that these benefits may be quintessential to trauma narrative writing.

The quotations below highlight the experiences of the authors within the study, demonstrating that this process had a counter-effect to the presupposed healing or other benefit of trauma writing when conducted outside of a structured approach overseen by a therapist. The first quotation speaks to this process reflectively, with the author conceding that even without a therapeutic scaffold being present, self-care steps should have been taken to manage the writing process. The second quotation additionally speaks to one of the author's experiences in conducting their writing while undertaking psychotherapy. This writing process, however, was not conducted under the care of a therapist, reiterating the possible issues present when undertaking a trauma narrative writing exercise outside of a structured, clinical approach.

So in hindsight, one of my main problems, I think, was that all of the advice you gave me about making sure that this process in the writing process was done in a managed, safe and structured environment, with my psychiatrist involved, and debriefing, I did not do at all. I think because I thought, 'Gosh, I don't want to think about it anymore than I have to', and if I have to sort of debrief and – it was like a total misunderstanding of the process ... I should have implemented more steps – self-care practices – into the writing process or the ruminating process, definitely (19 August 2020, transcript).

I never did any writing with her [my therapist]. I never really did anything she wanted me to do, because for me, it was like going once a week, dumping everything on her, compartmentalising it there and then doing my life. And then I'd go and dump on her and not have to think about it; that's how I used therapy. It was a compartmentalising exercise. ... I have since sent her a few things I've written about my mother, and my mother's illness and her death, which also can be categorised as [a] trauma narrative, as well, I believe. But I didn't do that for her and I didn't do that with her (19 August 2020, transcript).

Theme 3: Trauma narrative affect

This theme refers to the underlying experiences of feeling, emotion, or mood, as they relate to the trauma event or events, or the recounting of these events. In other words, to write, the authors speak to the need to be immersed in the story, and the data analysis highlights the effect of this immersion on the authors as it relates to the traumatic event/s that were being written about. The authors reflect on how, at time of writing the narratives, they were essentially transported back into the trauma to be able to write about it. This theme links with theme two (divergent from narrative therapy) as it highlights possible issues of undertaking such a task without a therapeutic scaffold.

The quotations included below additionally speak to the benefit of being able to retrieve the traumatic event through narrative, with the author questioning what the ongoing suppression or avoidance of that traumatic experience would continue to do to their physical and emotional wellbeing.

> Was the writing healing? It was more sort of surprising, really. I didn't feel like I had to heal. It was more a surprise that I got it into cogent little moments on the page. When I read *Black tulip* a few weeks ago, I also had a look at *Home* again and read through it; and I can flip right back to those moments. They're very authentic to me. Even though there's a bit in there where I say the therapist told me I couldn't remember [some of the event details] because I was protecting myself as a kid, but now that I've regained them, they're really real and sort of vibrant to me, those moments. The one when I'm a baby in a high chair and I can remember the beads on the high chair, and the kitchen, and the yellow jug with the black lid, and my mum. I just can remember all of that, like it's a scene from a movie. Each one of those moments at home, they're like scenes from a movie for me now (19 August 2020, transcript).

> And I don't dwell on them, I don't think about them; I didn't think about them before [the writing] … – but I guess in a way, Anna, our writing of this is like a safety valve, so in a way we're kind of privileged to be able to do be able to do that. I'm wondering if we couldn't do that, what that would do to our bodies and our minds (19 August 2020, transcript).

Theme 4: Agency and transparency

The theme of agency and transparency speaks to the authors enacting their agency to protect themselves when writing about trauma. This can be seen as enacting an ethic of (self) care by controlling what is revealed (see Wall 2008; Ellis 1999) – that is, limiting the explorations of their personal trauma 'as a way of mitigating [psychosomatic] vulnerability' (Holman Jones et al. 2013: 24). The process and writing of autoethnography potentially exposes the researcher to harm, and to conduct and present autoethnography well and rigorously may well be

Anna Denejkina

Sue Joseph

damaging (Denejkina 2021: 186). This is due to the interrogation of the self and through the process of exposing those secrets and histories, not only to the reader, but also to the researcher.

The quotations below demonstrate the use of self-censoring by the authors as a protective mechanism and an ethics of self-care; the use of their trauma narrative to regain agency by way of validating the traumatic experiences; and how these choices are made not as stylistic choices but as deliberate choices for the authors.

> There [were] definitely some things that I actively said I would not write about at all. There was definitely censoring (because this is touching on my family) so I was trying to limit how much I exposed my family in that story (19 August 2020, transcript).

> And the other question I just wanted to reflect on is how can we measure if the writing is healing? How do we know? For me, is it maybe perhaps more about acknowledging what had happened and validating those experiences? People invalidate a lot of traumatic experiences, so people's reactions could be [that] they didn't see it, [and therefore questioning you with] 'are you overreacting?' [This] diminishes what occurred and [suggests] that you're just having a strong reaction to something that you shouldn't, perhaps (19 August 2020, transcript).

> Everything that's happening in your household, especially when you're a child, that's what you see as normal and real, and you imagine this is what everyone deals with. And I think obviously a lot of those things are unresolved for me, but I think just writing all of that – even when I think about it now – it's so important to acknowledge that what happened should not have happened, and so then validate those experiences as negative experiences, as traumatic experiences, because we sort of grew up thinking this is completely normal (19 August 2020, transcript).

> So clearly it wasn't a stylistic decision. I think because the last section, for me, I can still remember the terror of being in that house that day, and the night, and I can still see his eyes, and I can still remember my father coming home, thank God. I don't know why I wrote it in second person; maybe I couldn't write it in first, I couldn't imagine it was me. I didn't do it to make the readership come with me at all, either. It wasn't stylistic. I think I had to remove myself from [the traumatic event by writing in second person] (19 August 2020, transcript).

Theme 5: Process of uncovering content for writing

The final theme identified in the transcript speaks to the varied processes undertaken by the authors of recovering or coming to terms with the traumatic events for the purpose of writing trauma narratives and the outcomes of these processes.

18   Copyright 2022-1. Ethical Space: The International Journal of Communication Ethics. All rights reserved. Vol 20, No 1 2023

The quotations below highlight different processes of uncovering content for trauma narrative, all outlining the difficulties within this process and how the authors continued to employ an ethic of self-care in the process of writing and working through the traumatic memories. This theme additionally highlights through the quotations below the issues that come to the surface when trauma narrative writing is undertaken outside a clinical scaffold, with the second quote particularly speaking to regression while ruminating on their childhood trauma.

> You know, the drowning scene, I do remember going to his house one day and his stepdaughter ran out and said: 'Oh, Rick's just told us about when he drowned you.' And I'd forgotten about it, and I sort of went in, sat down, had half a cup of coffee, went home, couldn't speak, and wrote a [fictional] scene about drowning for something else (which I never published), so I drew on that for the drowning scene there. But he did read that, and he was appalled. I think he was more appalled that I had remembered it the way I remembered it, which was a very traumatic experience, remembering drowning. I was four (19 August 2020, transcript).

> I think because the traumas I'm writing about, if you don't heal from them when you think about them, you regress back to that age. So for me, when I was five, when I think about those events, I think of them as a five-year-old – not as an adult, which is so strange – but that's where that memory stuck, and the way I process it is still as a child, I think (19 August 2020, transcript).

> When I remember family scenes my brother is not in it. When I remember driving in the car to go on holidays my older brother's not there, although he was. When I remember sitting down at the dining room table he's not there, although he was. But I couldn't find him – which is why I started seeing a therapist after I recovered this drowning scene – and then she just said: 'You've remembered three or four – I can't even remember how many; four, maybe, is the figure – moments in your life of deep trauma and terror perpetrated by your brother before you were 12 years old. There's really no reason to find out any more, you've got enough, you know how bad it was, and yes, it was deeply traumatic.' And I remember being really cross with her, and thinking: 'No, I want to know everything.'… And very shortly after that I remember thinking, 'Thank God I don't have to do that anymore and remember everything; I don't actually want to remember more.' So maybe in my head I'm thinking maybe that's all there was, knowing that it probably isn't, but you know, I was very busy, I had my kids and my job and my parents, and it was enough, I think (19 August 2020, transcript).

Copyright 2023-1. Ethical Space: The International Journal of Communication Ethics. All rights reserved. Vol 20, No 1 2023   **19**

Anna Denejkina

Sue Joseph

Discussion

This study was conducted through the process of collaborative reflection, using reflexivity to consider future applications of narrative writing as trauma intervention *outside* a manualised or structured approach overseen by a therapist or lay-therapist. Both authors wrote their narratives outside of a clinical setting – one as a PhD candidate and one as a creative researcher. Results from this study suggest that narrative exposure therapy outside a manualised (and/or clinical) setting has potential risk, and we caution the depiction or representation of trauma narrative as healing and applicable to all cases of trauma narrative writing.

Entering the process of trauma narrative writing without a therapeutic framework or scaffold does not necessarily equate to a healing intervention and, therefore, should not be equated with or positioned with research which supports this outcome when a therapeutic or manualised process is involved, until robust evidence is available on its efficacy.

The data additionally suggest that trauma narrative writing outside of the therapeutic framework can and is used as a way to recover or regain the agency of the writer. This positive outcome from the study, however, should *not* be equated to narrative trauma writing performing as a healing intervention outside of a therapeutic framework or scaffold, and should not replace this process.

Limitations

The results of this qualitative study are based on the thematic analysis of data from two researchers' written works and their reflection on these works. This study was conducted after the works were completed and, therefore, it was not possible to do a pre- and post-test using any psychometric measures on the participants to attempt to quantify any changes related to post-traumatic stress before and after writing the narratives. These results are exploratory in nature, and an extension of this paper's results will be useful in answering if and how narrative writing on traumatic experiences can be healing if conducted outside of a clinical or manualised framework. To answer this question, future research application of these exploratory findings for a possible randomised controlled trial using appropriate psychometric measures is needed to: (1) evaluate trauma narrative writing impact outside of a manualised or therapeutic framework; (2) develop processes for harm mitigation; and (3) provide data needed to determine its efficacy as potential healing intervention.

Conclusion

Writing from both a medical and a humanities approach, this paper set out to analyse any positive effects of narrative writing as an intervention for post-traumatic stress *without* clinical surrounds or a rigorous therapeutic scaffold. Through collaborative reflection, the authors interview each other and task each other to consider their state of mind and affect in the rendering of their work. Five themes emerge from the interview data, and of those five, only one has an implicit benefit of agency and transparency. The findings suggest that it is not implicit that writing trauma narrative has a beneficial impact on an author.

This paper goes some way in interrogating the notion of writing therapy as implicitly beneficial when rendering trauma narrative. Much care must be taken when undertaking this form of writing without a rigorous therapeutic scaffold, particularly within the tertiary HDR sector where its proliferation becomes a fraught ethical question in the commodifying of trauma narrative without due concern to mental health and well-being of research candidates and their supervisors. This is a separate issue to the rendering of trauma narrative outside an HDR setting, where due care and caution must be undertaken, again to safeguard an author's well-being.

Declaration of interest statement

No potential competing interest is reported by the authors.

References

Aristotle (1961) *Aristotle's poetics*, trans. Butcher, Samuel Henry, New York, Hill and Wang

Benish, Steven, Imel, Zac and Wampold, Bruce (2008) The relative efficacy of bona fide psychotherapies for treating post-traumatic stress disorder: A meta-analysis of direct comparisons, *Clin Psychol Rev.*, Vol. 28, No. 5 pp 746-758

Bjoroy, Anja, Madigan, Stephen and Nylund, David (2016) The practice of therapeutic letter writing in narrative therapy, Douglas, Barbara, Woolfe, Ray, Strawbridge, Sheelagh, Kasket, Elaine and Galbraith, Victoria (eds) *The handbook of counselling psychology*, California, Sage, fourth edition pp 332-348

Bolton, Gillian (2005) Introduction: Writing cures, Howlett, Stephanie, Lago, Colin and Wright, Jeannie (eds) *Writing cures: An introductory handbook of writing in counselling and psychotherapy,* London, Routledge pp 1-4

Braun, Virginia and Clarke, Victoria (2012) Thematic analysis, Cooper, Harris, Camic, Paul, Long, Debra, Panter, Abigail, Rindskopf, David and Sher, Kenneth (eds) *APA handbook of research methods in psychology, Vol. 2. Research designs: Quantitative, qualitative, neuropsychological, and biological*, Washington, American Psychological Association pp 57-71, DOI 10.1037/13620-004

Caizzi, Cristina (2012) Embodied trauma: Using the subsymbolic mode to access and change script protocol in traumatized adults, *Transactional Analysis Journal*, Vol. 42, No. 3 pp 165-175, DOI 10.1177/036215371204200302

Caruth, Cathy (1996) *Unclaimed experience: Trauma, narrative, and history*, Baltimore, Johns Hopkins University Press

Courtois, Christine (2004) Complex trauma, complex reactions: Assessment and treatment, *Psychotherapy: Theory, Research, Practice, Training,* Vol. 41, No. 4 pp 412-425, DOI 10.1037/0033-3204.41.4.412

Denejkina, Anna (2017) Exo-autoethnography: An introduction, *Forum Qualitative Sozialforschung* [*Forum: Qualitative Social Research*], Vol. 18, No. 3, DOI 10.17169/fqs-18.3.2754

Anna Denejkina

Sue Joseph

Denejkina, Anna (2019) Black tulip, in *Impact of intergenerational trauma transmission on the first post-Soviet generation*, PhD thesis, University of Technology Sydney pp 198-288. Available online at https://opus.lib.uts.edu.au/handle/10453/133342

Denejkina, Anna (2021) Exo-autoethnography as method for research on intergenerational trauma transmission, Holman Jones, Stacey, Adams, Tony and Ellis, Carolyn (eds) *Handbook of autoethnography*, London, Routledge pp 179-187

Ellis, Carolyn, Adams, Tony and Bochner, Arthur (2011) Autoethnography: An overview, *Forum Qualitative Sozialforschung [Forum: Qualitative Social Research]*, Vol. 12, No. 1, DOI 10.17169/fqs-12.1.1589

Ellis, Carolyn and Bochner, Arthur (2000) Autoethnography, personal narrative, reflexivity: Researcher as subject, Denzin, Norman and Lincoln, Yvonna (eds) *Handbook of qualitative research*, California, Sage, second edition pp 733-769

Esterling, Brian, L'Abate, Luciano, Murray, Edward and Pennebaker, James (1999) Empirical foundations for writing in prevention and psychotherapy: Mental and physical health outcomes, *Clin Psychol Rev*, Vol. 19, No. 1 pp 79-96

Gwozdziewycz, Nicholas and Mehl-Madrona, Lewis (2013) Meta-analysis of the use of narrative exposure therapy for the effects of trauma among refugee populations, *The Permanente Journal*, Vol. 17, No. 1 pp 70-76, DOI 10.7812/TPP/12-058

Harris, Judith (2003) The necessity of mourning: Psychoanalytic paradigms for change and tansformation in the composition classroom, *College English*, Vol. 65, No. 6 pp 668-675

Haynes, Kathryn (2017) Autoethnography in accounting research, Hoque, Zahirul, Parker, Lee, Covaleski, Mark and Haynes, Kathryn (eds) *Routledge companion to qualitative accounting research methods*, London, Routledge pp 215-230

Hirai, Michiyo, Dolma, Serkan, Vernon, Laura and Clum, George (2020) A longitudinal investigation of the efficacy of online expressive writing interventions for Hispanic students exposed to traumatic events: competing theories of action, *Psychology & Health*, Vol. 35, No. 12 pp 1459-1476, DOI 10.1080/08870446.2020.1758324

Hoge, Charles W. (2011) Interventions for war-related post-traumatic stress disorder, *JAMA*, Vol. 306, No. 5 pp 549-551, DOI 10.1001/jama.2011.1096

Jacob, Nadja, Neuner, Frank, Maedl, Anna, Schaal, Susanne and Elbert, Thomas (2014) Dissemination of psychotherapy for trauma spectrum disorders in postconflict settings: a randomized controlled trial in Rwanda, *Psychotherapy and Psychosomatics*, Vol. 83, No. 6 pp 354-363, DOI 10.1159/000365114

Joseph, Sue (2013) *Home*, Hamilton, Paula and Ashton, Paul (eds) *Locating suburbia: Memory, place, creativity*, Sydney, UTSePress pp 103-123

Kearney, Richard (2008) Narrating pain: The ethics of catharsis, Sullivan, Sharon and Schmidt, Dennis (eds) *Difficulties of ethical life*, New York, Fordham University Press pp 181-194

Landless, Bronwen, Walker, Melissa and Kaimal, Girija (2019) Using human and computer-based text analysis of clinical notes to understand military service members' experiences with therapeutic writing, *The Arts in Psychotherapy*, Vol. 62, February pp 77-84, DOI 10.1016/j.aip.2018.10.002

Lange, Alfred, Schrieken, Bart, van de Ven, Jean-Pierre, Bredeweg, Bert, Emmelkamp, Paul, van der Kilk, Joisel, Lydsdottier, Linda, Massaro, Marina and Reuvers, Anneke (2000) 'Interapy': The effects of a short protocolled treatment of post-traumatic stress and pathological grief through the internet, *Behavioral and Cognitive Psychotherapy*, Vol. 28, No. 2 pp 175-192

Lange-Nielsen, Ida Ingridsdatter, Kolltveit, Silje, Thabet, Abdul Aziz Mousa, Dyregrov, Atle, Pallesen, Ståle, Johnsen, Tom Backer and Laberg, J. C. (2012) Short-term effects of a writing intervention among adolescents in Gaza, *Journal of Loss and Trauma: International Perspectives on Stress & Coping*, Vol. 17, No. 5 pp 403-422, DOI 10.1080/15325024.2011.650128

Lely, Jeanette, Smid, Geert, Jongedijk, Ruud, Knipscheer, Jeroen and Kleber, Rolf (2019) The effectiveness of narrative exposure therapy: A review, meta-analysis and meta-regression analysis, *European Journal of Psychotraumatology*, Vol. 10, No. 1, DOI 10.1080/20008198.2018.1550344

Lengelle, Reinekke and Meijers, Frans (2009) Mystery to mastery: An exploration of what happens in the black box of writing and healing, *Journal of Poetry Therapy*, Vol. 22, No. 2 pp 57-75

Littrell, Jill (2009) Expression of emotion: When it causes trauma and when it helps, *Journal of Evidence-based Social Work*, Vol. 6, No. 3 pp 300-320

Merriam-Webster (n.d.) Catharsis in *Merriam-Webster.com dictionary*. Available online at https://www.merriam-webster.com/dictionary/catharsis

Neuner, Frank, Catani, Claudia, Ruf, Martina, Schauer, Elisabeth, Schauer, Maggie and Elbert, Thomas (2008) Narrative exposure therapy for the treatment of traumatized children and adolescents (KidNET): From neurocognitive theory to field intervention, *Child and adolescent psychiatric clinics of North America*, Vol. 17, No. 3 pp 641-664

O'Hanlon, Bill (1994) The third wave, *Networker*, Vol. 18, No. 6 pp 19-29

Pascoe, Phaedra E. (2016) Using patient writings in psychotherapy: Review of evidence for expressive writing and cognitive behavioral writing therapy, *The American Journal of Psychiatry Residents' Journal*, Vol. 11, No. 3 pp 3-6

Payne, Martin (2006) *Narrative therapy: An introduction for counsellors*, California, Sage

Pennebaker, James and Beall, Sandra (1986) Confronting a traumatic event: Toward an understanding of inhibition and disease, *Journal of Abnormal Psychology*, Vol. 95, No. 3 pp 274-281

Pennebaker, James (2000) Telling stories: The health benefits of narrative, *Literature and Medicine*, Vol. 19, No. 1 pp 3-18

Perrella, Raffaella, Del Villano, Nadia and Caviglia, Giorgio (2016) Referential activity, dissociation, psychopathology and psychotherapy, *Research in Psychotherapy: Psychopathology, Process and Outcome*, Vol. 19, No. 2 pp 165-171, DOI 10.4081/ripppo.2016.243

Phillips, Lynne and Rolfe, Alison (2016) Words that work? Exploring client writing in therapy, *Counselling and Psychotherapy Research*, Vol. 16, No.3 pp 193-200

Phoenix Australia (2020) *Australian guidelines for the prevention and treatment of acute stress disorder, post-traumatic stress disorder and complex PTSD*, Phoenix Australia, Centre for Post-traumatic Mental Health. Available online at https://www.phoenixaustralia.org/australian-guidelines-for-ptsd/

Ramsey-Wade, Christine, Williamson, Heidi and Meyrick, Jane (2020) Therapeutic writing for disordered eating: A systematic review, *Journal of Creativity in Mental Health*, Vol. 16, No. 1 pp 59-79, DOI 10.1080/15401383.2020.1760988

Robjant, Katy and Fazel, Mina (2010) The emerging evidence for Narrative Exposure Therapy: A review, *Clinical Psychology Review*, Vol. 30, No. 8 pp 1030-1039, DOI 10.1016/j.cpr.2010.07.004

Schauer, Maggie, Neuner, Frank and Elbert, Thomas (2011) *Narrative exposure therapy. A short-term intervention for traumatic stress disorders after war, terror or torture*, Massachusetts, Hogrefe & Huber, second, expanded edition

Singer, Jefferson, Singer, Bruce and Berry, Meredith (2013) A meaning-based intervention for addiction: Using Narrative Therapy and mindfulness to treat alcohol abuse, Hicks, Joshua and Routledge, Clay (eds) *The experience of meaning in life*, Berlin, Springer pp 379-391, DOI 10.1007/978-94-007-6527-628

Sloan, Denise, Sawyer, Alice, Lowmaster, Sara, Wernick, Jeremy and Marx, Brian (2015) Efficacy of narrative writing as an Intervention for PTSD: Does the evidence support its use? *Journal of Contemporary Psychotherapy*, Vol. 45, No. 4 pp 215-225, DOI 10.1007/s10879-014-9292-x

Sloan, Denise, Marx, Brian, Bovin, Michelle, Feinstein, Brian and Gallagher, Matthew (2012) Written exposure as an intervention for PTSD: A randomized clinical trial with motor vehicle accident survivors, *Behav Res Ther*. Vol. 50, No. 10 pp 627-635

Smyth, Joshua, Hockemeyer, Jill and Tulloch, Heather (2008) Expressive writing and post traumatic stress disorder: Effects on trauma symptoms, mood states, and cortisol reactivity, *British Journal of Health Psychology*, Vol. 13, No. 1 pp 85-93

Copyright 2023-1. Ethical Space: The International Journal of Communication Ethics. All rights reserved. Vol 20, No 1 2023

Anna Denejkina

Sue Joseph

Steele, Emily, Wood, David, Usadi, Eva and Applegarth, Michael (2018) TRR's warrior camp: An Intensive treatment program for combat trauma in active military and veterans of all eras, *Military Medicine*, Vol. 183, supplement 1 pp 403-407, DOI 10.1093/milmed/usx153

Steinberg, Derek (2005) From archetype to impressions: The magic of words, Bolton, Gillie, Howlett, Stephanie, Lago, Colin and Wright, Jeannie (eds) *Writing cures: An introductory handbook of writing in counselling and psychotherapy,* London, Routledge pp 44-56

Stenmark, Hakon, Catani, Claudia, Neuner, Frank, Elbert, Thomas and Holen, Are (2013) Treating PTSD in refugees and asylum seekers within the general health care system. A randomized controlled multicenter study, *Behav Res Ther*, Vol. 51, No. 10 pp 641-647

Tedeschi, Richard and Calhoun, Lawrence (1996) The post-traumatic growth inventory: Measuring the positive legacy of trauma, *Journal of Traumatic Stress*, Vol. 9, No. 3 pp 455-471

Tedeschi, Richard and Calhoun, Lawrence (2004) Post-traumatic growth: Conceptual foundations and empirical evidence, *Psychological Inquiry*, Vol. 15, No. 1 pp 1-18

Van der Kolk, Bessel (2014) *The body keeps the score*, London, Penguin Books

Van Emmerik, Arnold, Kamphuis, Jan H. and Emmelkamp, Paul (2008) Treating acute stress disorder and posttraumatic stress disorder with cognitive behavioral therapy or structured writing therapy: A randomized controlled trial, *Psychotherapy and Psychosomatics*, Vol. 77, No. 2 pp 93-100

White, Michael and Epston, David (1990) *Narrative means to therapeutic ends,* New York, W. W. Norton

Wright, Jeannie and Chung, Man, Cheung (2001) Mastery or mystery? Therapeutic writing: A review of the literature, *British Journal of Guidance & Counselling*, Vol. 29, No.3 pp 277-291, DOI 10.1080/03069880120073003

Data availability statement

Due to the nature of this research, participants of this study did not agree for their data to be shared publicly, so supporting data is not available.

Note on the contributors

Dr Anna Denejkina is a lecturer in the Graduate Research School and member of the Translational Health Research Institute (THRI) and Young and Resilient Research Centre, Western Sydney University. Dr Denejkina's research focuses on intergenerational trauma transmission, specifically in military families.

Sue Joseph (PhD), a journalist for more than forty years in Australia and the UK, began working as an academic, teaching print journalism at the University of Technology Sydney in 1997. As a Senior Lecturer, she taught in journalism and creative writing, particularly creative non-fiction writing. Now as Associate Professor, she is a Senior Research Fellow at the University of South Australia and is a doctoral supervisor at the University of Sydney, Central Queensland University and the University of Technology Sydney. Her fourth book, *Behind the text: Candid conversations with Australian creative nonfiction writers*, was published in 2016. She is currently Joint Editor of *Ethical Space: The International Journal of Communication Ethics* and former Special Issues Editor of *TEXT Journal of Writing and Writing Courses*. She is co-editor of the scholarly collection of essays about memoir *Mediating memory: Tracing the limits of memoir*, published by Routledge in 2018, and *Still here: Memoirs of trauma, illness and loss*, also published by Routledge (2019); and with Richard Lance Keeble, co-editor of *Profile pieces: Journalism and the 'human interest' bias* published by Routledge (2015), *Profiling handbook* published by Abramis Academic (2015); and *Sex and journalism: Critical, global perspectives*, published by Bite-sized Books (2019).

Carl Fox
Joe Saunders
John Steel
Julie Firmstone
Charlotte Elliott-Harvey
Martin Conboy
Jane Mulderrig

What is the purpose of a code of ethics for the press?

Journalism plays a crucial role in democratic societies, but the ability of journalists to perform that role is jeopardised by a profound crisis of trust in the profession. One response often employed by press councils is to refresh their code of ethics, but what purpose do such codes serve and can they make any difference to how journalists actually behave or relate to the public? Drawing on Jonathan Wolff's idea of 'engaged philosophy', we outline the problems to which codes may be an answer and provide a taxonomy of the purposes they may then fulfil. We lay out four possible roles for codes and argue they can all make a worthwhile contribution to raising press standards and justifying higher levels of public trust. We substantiate our discussion by examining the codes of ethics of press councils in twelve European countries, along with the IMPRESS and IPSO codes in the UK, to determine which of these functions they are explicitly intended to serve. We conclude that there is scope to make greater use of codes to improve the ethical culture in newsrooms.

Key words: codes of ethics, trust, press standards, press regulation, freedom of the press, journalism ethics

Introduction
What is the point of a code of ethics? Any self-respecting press council will have one, but what purpose are they intended to serve and what effects may they actually have on the practice of journalists and

Carl Fox

Joe Saunders

John Steel

Julie Firmstone

Charlotte Elliott-
Harvey

Martin Conboy

Jane Mulderrig

the quality of their relationship to the public? The role and value of professional codes of ethics within journalism has long been contested and debated within media studies scholarship. From Mary Cronin and James McPherson's (1995) historical study of state press association codes from the 1920s, and Lee Wilkins and Bonnie Brennan's (2004) analysis of the American Society of Newspaper Editors' and the American Newspaper Guild's codes in the 1920s and 30s, to expansive comparative studies of ethics codes and their use around the world (Laitila 1995; Hafez 2002; Himelboim and Limor 2008), codes of press ethics have long been the subject of concerted academic interest.

As Bertrand (2005: 9) acknowledges, it is easy to be cynical about media accountability in general, and this is particularly true of codes of ethics. Many believe, as Beyerstein (1993: 417) puts it, that 'codes of ethics exist primarily to make professions look moral, not to promote morality in the profession'.[1] Indeed, in the specific case of the press, studies have shown that codes of ethics can be neglected by journalists and often act primarily as a marker for professional identity and credibility (Pritchard and Morgan 1989; Himelboim and Limor 2008). An even more worrying possibility is that not only are codes of no particular help in raising standards, they may even be positively harmful. Codes may serve to present a respectable front and thus engender and exploit unwarranted trust from an unsuspecting public.

This concern feeds into a wider crisis of trust in journalism.[2] According to the Reuters Institute Digital News Report for 2021, only 44 per cent of people trust the news media in general and exactly half trust the news sources that they themselves use.[3] These figures interrupt a downward trend and constitute a modest recovery from previous years – which is likely a result of the pandemic – but still remain alarmingly low. As faith in the profession ebbs away, it seems reasonable to worry that journalists will find it progressively more difficult to perform the traditional roles ascribed to them in a representative system of democracy. How effectively can journalists inform a public that is disinclined to listen to them, or hold powerful figures to account if the questions they ask are dismissed as biased?[4] So, how can trust be restored, and, more importantly, what would actually make trust in the press more justified? One strategy sometimes employed by standards organisations such as press councils is to double down on codes of ethics by writing new codes or revising existing ones in the hope that they will shore up public faith in the ethical commitments of the profession.[5] In this paper we adopt an applied ethics perspective to tackle the question of how codes could, and should, be used to ensure that trust is warranted.

One response in the applied ethics literature to widespread, and often well-founded, scepticism about codes has been to think more clearly about our expectations of them. That makes it possible to distinguish between different purposes they may serve (Frankel 1989; Beyerstein 1993). We adapt that approach for the context of journalism, laying out four distinct roles that codes of ethics can play.

- First, codes can be *action-guiding* when they offer normative guidance to practitioners.

- Second, they are *disciplinary* when they set out rules that are backed up by sanctions.

- Third, we describe them as *public-facing* when they are written to be consulted by the public and offer a set of standards against which they can evaluate the performance of the press.

- Finally, codes of ethics are *identity-forming* if they lay a foundation for a professional identity, and thereby embed ethical principles into the way journalists understand and value their own social role.

We argue that, although each of these functions has limitations, they can all make some contribution to improving the conduct of journalists and, thereby, raise levels of confidence in the trustworthiness of the press. We then turn to examine the codes of ethics of the twelve top-ranked European countries in the World Press Freedom Index to determine which of these functions they are actually intended to serve. As our project is focused on learning lessons for the UK context, we also look at the codes of ethics from the two main UK press regulation bodies, IMPRESS and IPSO. As we shall see, it is notable that few codes explicitly aim to be public-facing, and none at all claim that they are building or buttressing a distinctive ethical identity for journalists. Although it is important not to overstate the significance of codes of ethics, we conclude that there is scope to make greater use of codes than we currently do to build and maintain an ethical culture in newsrooms.

We will begin with some reflections on our method and the broader context in which this research has been conducted, before turning to the task of outlining the four main purposes that we think codes of ethics can, and should, serve for the press. Our next section then applies this framework to our chosen countries, while we end with our conclusions.

Method

This paper forms one part of a wider inter-disciplinary research project bringing together expertise from applied ethics, journalism studies, applied linguistics and law to explore how 'freedom of the press' is defined, codified, articulated, practised and understood in European countries where this ideal is strongly embedded.[6] The analysis of press codes is the first stage of our study which, overall, intends to provide a rich understanding of how codes, among other contributing factors,[7] may contribute to an ethical press culture by exploring them both from a philosophical perspective and through the perceptions and experiences of news workers and other stakeholders.[8] One of the main objectives of the project is to assess what practical lessons can then be applied to the UK context.

Carl Fox

Joe Saunders

John Steel

Julie Firmstone

Charlotte Elliott-
Harvey

Martin Conboy

Jane Mulderrig

Much of the valuable work that has been done on journalistic codes of ethics takes a primarily descriptive approach, comparing and contrasting the content of various codes (Roberts 2012; Limor and Himelboim 2006; Himelboim and Limor 2008; Cooper 1990; Laitila 1995).[9] However, as Ward (2015: 13) observes, the ethics of journalism is a sub-species of ethics understood more broadly.[10] The subject matter of ethics is the question of how to live better lives. This means that codes of ethics can also be explored as part of the philosophical project to work out how journalism can, and *ought,* to be practised in order for us all to live better.

The applied ethics contribution to the project is guided by Jonathan Wolff's idea of 'engaged philosophy', which 'starts from the problems we perceive in the world as it is and considers how philosophical thinking can help us to make improvements' (2020: 259). The reason why Wolff (2020: 6) calls his approach 'engaged philosophy' rather than 'applied ethics' is because even though applied ethics typically aims to address pressing problems, he wants to avoid the lingering idea that philosophical explorations of political and social issues ought to be conducted apart from the messy complications presented by such problems – in the armchair – and then later 'applied' to solve them.[11] By outlining the problems to which codes may be an answer and providing a new taxonomy of the purposes that they may then fulfil, our analysis deploys Wolff's 'problem-first' method to furnish additional conceptual tools for anyone interested in understanding and evaluating both the operation and potential of existing codes and, indeed, in designing new ones.

This approach is complemented by another insight about the value of general philosophical thinking in debates about public policy. As Hales (2011: 227) argues, clarifying concepts, making distinctions, identifying fallacious inferences and so on are central to a philosophical approach and can help to illuminate the underlying principles that are at stake in a debate.[12] Wolff (2020: 269) concurs and notes that these philosophical skills are especially helpful when trying to frame an issue for discussion. Distinguishing between the various challenges that codes may be employed to solve facilitates our ability to take a step back and reflect on the purpose of codes more effectively. Relatedly, outlining specific functions that they may then be deployed to serve helps us to see which underlying ethical values we may use them to pursue. With this foundation in place, the empirical observations we later make allow us to draw some conclusions about the prospects for making better use of codes of ethics.

We examined the press council codes from the twelve top-ranked European countries from the 2018 Reporters Without Borders (RSF) World Press Freedom Index, plus the two codes from the press regulators IMPRESS and IPSO in the UK.[13] We were generally able to source English translations of the press councils' codes of ethics from each country's press council website. However, English translations were requested from the press councils in Austria, Belgium[14] (*Raad voor de Journalistiek*), and Sweden. Professional translations were acquired for the codes of ethics from Belgium (*Conseil de Déontologie Journalistique*) and the Slovak Republic.

Four roles for codes of ethics

Let us start with a basic question: what exactly is a code of ethics? We define a code of ethics as a formal statement of moral principles to which some identifiable group of people are expected to adhere in the course of their work. Scholars working on codes often presuppose that the purpose of making a formal statement of moral principles is to guide the behaviour of the members of that group, and so build that directly into their definitions.[15] However, as Frankel (1989: 111) points out, codes can serve a range of overlapping functions. In this section, we lay out four distinct roles that we believe that codes of ethics can, and indeed should, aim to play. This is not meant to be an exhaustive list, but rather to capture the most important ways that codes can respond to real-world problems affecting journalists.[16]

Action-guiding

Ward (2010: 15) identifies a basic problem with which all journalists will be familiar. It is often not obvious what the right thing to do is, and difficult situations 'present us with a "knot" of facts, potential consequences, options and rival values'. Codes can simply aim to tell unsure practitioners about what they should and should not do in the course of their work. This is the most intuitive purpose to which a code of ethics can be put.

Action-guiding codes thus intend to make a difference by offering authoritative advice. Looking at our sample of codes of ethics, we found that they all aimed to play an action-guiding role. Every one of them contained requirements and proscriptions. However, many of these could have been predicted by anyone with a passing interest in journalism. For example, would even a novice journalist have to consult their code of ethics to discover whether they are expected to offer the subjects of their stories a right to reply? Action-guiding codes purport to be worthwhile because they assist practitioners in making difficult decisions, but they would fail to achieve this goal if all they do is restate what is already considered common sense.

A related concern is that codes fail to guide action because they are too vague. As an example, take this paragraph from Section C.1 of the Guidelines of the Netherlands Press Council: a publication 'must not infringe the privacy of persons any more than is reasonably required within the framework of this report. An intrusion of privacy would be imprudent if not in reasonable proportion to the social interest of the publication'. One is compelled to ask what counts as reasonable. Opinions on that will differ, and so one could object that it is hard to see how much guidance is really being offered.

Carl Fox

Joe Saunders

John Steel

Julie Firmstone

Charlotte Elliott-
Harvey

Martin Conboy

Jane Mulderrig

However, across the codes there were also numerous instances of more focused advice that we thought a journalist would plausibly find informative and useful. As an example, we can take Guideline 8.5 from the German Press Council code: 'The names and photographs of missing persons may be published, however only in agreement with the responsible authorities.' If a German journalist was unsure about whether it were permissible to publish the name or photograph of a missing person, then consulting their code would prove helpful as it not only answers that question, but also stipulates the concrete steps that they should take before doing so.

Now, this is both a strength and a potential weakness for the position that codes should be action-guiding. That there are some instances when codes do provide helpful advice proves that this is possible. This is a potential weakness, though, because it gives rise to another possible worry. If codes are expected to provide detailed guidance then the impression may form that anything that is not specifically ruled out by a code is, therefore, permissible (Beauchamp and Childress 1994: 7). On encountering an eventuality that is not covered by the code, a journalist may feel that they have licence to treat the lack of specificity as a loophole and proceed however they wish.

Of course, it would be a mistake to think that action-guiding codes could create moral loopholes. The concern is that given what we know about human psychology, this is a sufficiently likely reaction that it renders any attempt to give precise guidance unwise. We think this concern is overblown. It is a relatively easy fix to acknowledge that a code cannot anticipate every conceivable situation in which a practitioner may find herself. Moreover, although there is little doubt that some will seek to exploit the lacunae in the letter of any code, we see no reason to be fatalistic about the capacity of journalists as a group to interpret general principles and to prioritise the spirit of a code. This objection does serve to illustrate, however, that codes cannot hope to provide all the answers. Action-guiding codes can be of some use, but they are not a substitute for good judgment.

It is also worth acknowledging that there is an important promissory note in play whenever codes set out to guide action. It is never enough that a code says that someone should behave in such and such a way. Their authority is only legitimate when the practitioner has good reasons to defer to the code. The content of a code must thus be suitably *justified*, and those justifications must be available for scrutiny, reflection, and, potentially, revision.

Disciplinary

The weight of moral considerations alone often fails to guarantee ethical behaviour. If the principles at stake are important then what should the journalist do? Codes of ethics are sometimes described as 'having teeth' when there is some mechanism for enforcing their provisions. Indeed, attaching meaningful punishments to violations of a code of ethics also sends out a signal that a code is not to be viewed as an aspirational document, but one that practitioners must take seriously in the here and now.

A related reason to impose tangible costs on practitioners who violate their code of ethics is the message that it can send on behalf of any parties who were wronged. To wrong someone is to treat them in a manner that is incompatible with their moral status. Thus, it involves showing them disrespect. This is particularly problematic if the individual or group concerned is already struggling against discrimination, exclusion or oppression. Public action in defence of their interests can be a powerful statement reasserting their status as moral and political equals, and can go some way towards repairing damage that may have been done to their social standing.

Enforcement of a code of ethics can take a number of forms. When it comes to the press, it is usually an order to publish a retraction, backed up by the possibility of financial penalties or the stigma of expulsion from the relevant standards organisation. These powers are sometimes grounded in legislation, as is the case in Denmark where the press council was established by the Media Liability Act of 1991. However, even though membership of most press councils is voluntary, so long as a member is not inclined to leave then they can be disciplined. This point is made explicitly in the preamble to the Austrian press council's code which states that newspapers and magazines that commit themselves to compliance with the principles of the code of ethics 'undertake to publish every and any finding of the Austrian Press Council directed against said newspaper or magazine and the publication of which the Council has required'.

Of course, how strict a disciplinary body is with its members depends on the degree to which it is prepared to prioritise the values enshrined in the code over the interests of those members. The effectiveness of a disciplinary code will thus be a function not only of the severity of the sanctions that stand behind it, but also the likelihood that they will be deployed.

Some of the problems we raised for action-guiding codes resurface for disciplinary codes. Frankel (1989: 111) makes the case that to serve a disciplinary function a code must include 'a set of detailed rules to govern professional conduct and to serve as the basis for adjudicating grievances'. To the degree that codes are vague and espouse general principles it is correspondingly difficult to convict someone of violating them, and the significance of potential loopholes increases when sanctions are threatened.

Though this is true, it is a bad argument for rejecting a disciplinary function for codes altogether. We wrestle with the same problems when writing and enforcing laws but nobody would suggest that passing

Carl Fox

Joe Saunders

John Steel

Julie Firmstone

Charlotte Elliott-Harvey

Martin Conboy

Jane Mulderrig

laws is a waste of time. The real questions when it comes to disciplinary codes of ethics are the thorny ones of substance and procedure. Are the rules we wish to see enforced good ones, and are they applied in a fair and transparent manner?

Public-facing

A different way to develop the notion that codes of ethics can be employed to address worries about the accountability of the press is to consider how they can provide not just practitioners or regulators with a statement of the commitments of the profession, but also members of the public. Since most of the traditional conceptions of the role of the press in democratic societies position the press as an institution that serves the people, there is an obvious attraction to furnishing them with a statement of what they are entitled to expect. The public would then have a better vantage point from which to critically evaluate the conduct of the press. Further, they would be empowered to find their own ways of holding journalists and media organisations to account. As Bertrand (2005: 5) argues, to move beyond regulation or self-regulation to true accountability, the public must be involved.

The idea that a press code of ethics should also be designed for public consumption is expressed in Section I.1.c of the code of ethics of the Association for the Protection of Journalistic Ethics in the Slovak Republic, which states that one of the purposes of the code is 'to inform the public of the ethical rules of journalistic practice'. Similar sentiments can also be found in the codes for Germany, the Netherlands and the UK (IMPRESS). Addressing the public directly makes it clear that it is not just a document to which they have access, but rather a resource that has been created *for* them.

Informing the public is one benefit of a transparent and accessible code, but we could be more ambitious and aim to include them in the process of writing the code in the first place. Culver (2017: 488) contends that efforts to improve accountability to the public 'would serve the twin goods of expanding journalists' understanding of the communities and publics they serve and promoting better public insight into the operations, responsibilities and practices of news media'.

Left to their own devices, any group of people will naturally be tempted to arrange things so that their lives will be easier. Public scrutiny of the press and, in particular, scrutiny conducted by underrepresented groups in our society, is just as important as press scrutiny of politicians and other powerful figures.

Identity-forming

Journalists face a range of pressures in the course of their work that make it more difficult to adhere to ethical principles. Is this something that a code of ethics could help to address? Foundational texts can sometimes shape how professions think of themselves. Medicine has a number of famous examples, with the Hippocratic Oath and the Helsinki Declaration[17] being the two most influential. To 'do no harm' is now simply a constitutive part of what it means to be a doctor. It may seem fanciful to suppose that a press council code of ethics could have the same kind of impact, but tapping into the power of identity provides another way that codes of ethics could be useful.[18] As we will discuss in the next section, the French and Swiss codes come closest to playing this role by employing language that implies the existence of a distinctive role-based identity that journalists ought to embrace. For instance, the French code expresses its rules as characteristics of a person and states that it is only by observing them that a 'journalist is worthy of his name'. In fact, there are two ways in which identity-formation can be helpful and they correspond to thinking about identity both on the level of the individual and the collective.

With regard to the former, internalising the principles of a code can make an enormous difference to how one relates to them. Think about something as simple as giving up your seat on the bus to someone who clearly needs it. This is a morally good thing to do. Indeed, it will often be obligatory, which is to say something that you ought to do. Faced with that kind of ethical demand, many of us will still have to think about it a little. We will have to remind ourselves that we should get up and offer the seat, and then we will have to overcome a degree of inertia before we eventually act. That's not a problem. We still get to the right outcome. However, it is *better* when offering your seat is just what *you* do in those circumstances. When that becomes a principle that forms part of your self-conception you will act more quickly and more decisively. Failing to do it will also seem more costly because it is a failure to live up to a moral principle that you have endorsed. It will thus be a source of shame, and shame can be an extremely powerful motivational force.[19]

The goal of an identity-forming code, on the individual level, would be to determine what it *means* to be a journalist. It would thus help bring about a state of affairs in which not publishing without a second source, or offering a right to reply, or distinguishing between news and comment would be something that a journalist just would not do. To even seriously contemplate it would be to step outside of the mindset of a committed journalist.[20] With this context in place we can see that the French National Syndicate of Journalists' code[21] contains a suggestive line: it is 'with these conditions that a journalist is worthy of his name'.[22] The idea here seems to be that a 'real' journalist is someone who conforms to the principles laid out in the code. The corollary would then be that anyone who fails to adhere to the code cannot really be a journalist and would be making a mistake in describing themselves as such. Although establishing such an identity for any group of people would not be easy, it does offer the potential for a form of genuine self-regulation in which practitioners monitor and discipline themselves on the basis of agreed principles. For that reason we think it merits serious consideration.

Carl Fox

Joe Saunders

John Steel

Julie Firmstone

Charlotte Elliott-Harvey

Martin Conboy

Jane Mulderrig

Identity-formation also has collective benefits. If a critical mass of people believe that some actions are incompatible with occupying the role of a journalist then that can provide a measure of protection from pressure to behave unethically. This is for two reasons. First, it makes asking a journalist to violate their code a far more consequential proposition. They will be giving up a valued identity and can expect to be ostracised from the community of journalists if the action ever comes to light. Depending on the character of the person making a morally problematic request, this may be enough to make them rethink it. Second, if an unscrupulous actor knows that it would be difficult to find anyone else to do whatever it is that a particular journalist is refusing to do, then there is no advantage in firing them. This rebalances the incentive structure of the situation in favour of the journalist and makes it easier for them to adhere to their ethical principles.

Schwartz (2001: 255) uses the metaphor of a shield to capture the thought that codes can provide some defence against underhanded requests and orders. Our suggestion is a little different in so far as the protection is not afforded directly by a code, but rather by one's confidence in one's colleagues and their commitment to a *shared* code. Laying claim to a professional title such as 'journalist', and benefiting from the positive associations that arise from the hard work and integrity of other journalists can, as Davis (1991: 167) argues, also create a duty of fairness to reciprocate. We could, therefore, describe the effect as a shield-wall rather than a shield.

This notion of solidarity can be developed to distinguish between two models of professionalisation. Attaining the status of a profession can set an occupation apart from other ways of making a living in ways that confer tangible and substantial benefits for practitioners such as self-regulation, control over entry to the ranks of the profession, and increased social standing and capital. However, these privileges will be undeserved if the profession does not have at its core a genuine – and motivationally efficacious – ethos of public service. So, professionalisation can be done primarily to serve the interests of the members, or it can be done for the sake of an important ethical goal. In fact, there is evidence that codes have a history of being used by journalists to rally around an ethical vision. Harcup (2020: 46) describes how the creation of the first National Union of Journalists' code of conduct for the UK and Ireland in 1936 was a 'bottom-up response to top-down pressure to sacrifice ethics for circulation'. No doubt, constructing (or reconstructing) this kind of shield-wall would be difficult, but the benefits could be considerable.

What the codes say about their purpose

Of course, no code of ethics would exist if its authors did not have some end (or ends) in mind and it is important to acknowledge the significance of unstated or implicit aims. For instance, one unacknowledged goal that many codes may be thought to serve is to professionalise a practice in the sense we discussed in the last section: namely of increasing its prestige by standardising it and creating the perception, if not always the reality, that its members are strongly committed to a set of ethical principles.[23] Codes do not exist in a vacuum, and their authors will sometimes be entitled to make assumptions about how the publication of a code will be interpreted by practitioners, government and the wider public. Identifying and untangling these unwritten assumptions is clearly of interest for what they can tell us about the dominant norms and beliefs that permeate a practice such as journalism. Leaving particular aims unspoken may also evince some cynicism on the part of the authors of some codes, if those aims are self-serving and use the appearance of a commitment to ethical values to facilitate immoral behaviour.

For these reasons it is clearly of interest not just what codes say about their roles, but what they leave unsaid. However, there are four reasons to focus on what codes say explicitly about their purpose, or purposes. First, we have attempted to show that codes can be a way to address a range of ethical problems. It is tempting to take a myopic view of codes and to think that they must all serve one single overarching purpose. Analysing codes by their stated function can help to illuminate the point that they can serve multiple purposes and, indeed, could be revised to serve others as well. Second, even though it may not tell the whole story, the aims stated in a code are an indication of what the authors intended the publication of the code to achieve. Third, as we have discussed, there is a range of potential audiences for a code. Its explicit goals can help to identify the target audience. This can eliminate confusion and help with expectation management for individuals outside the target audience who read the code. Finally, being clear about the genuine ethical challenges that a code is supposed to address can help to make it more likely that a code will actually be successful at achieving them. This is for the simple reason that it is only possible to directly pursue a goal if you know what it is. Codes of ethics only work when people make them work, so it is in everyone's interest that the intentions behind a code are communicated in a straightforward fashion.

In order to substantiate our discussion we, therefore, examined the codes of ethics listed above[24] to see what they said themselves about the purpose, or purposes, they aimed to serve. In this section we report our findings, which are summarised in Table 1:

Carl Fox

Joe Saunders

John Steel

Julie Firmstone

Charlotte Elliott-
Harvey

Martin Conboy

Jane Mulderrig

Table 1. Breakdown of codes by stated function

Country	Action-Guiding	Disciplinary	Public-Facing	Identity-Formation
Austria	X	X		
Belgium[25]	X			
Denmark	X	X		
Finland	X			
France[26]	X			
Germany	X	X	X	
Ireland	X	X		
Netherlands	X	X	X	
Norway	X			
Slovakia	X	X	X	
Sweden	X	X		
Switzerland	X			
UK (IMPRESS)	X	X	X	
UK (IPSO)	X	X		

Our first finding was that categorising the codes proved to be more challenging than we anticipated. In fact, only two codes – Slovakia and UK (IMPRESS) – contained a section or subsection dedicated to setting out the purposes of the code. This generated ambiguity about the purpose of some of the codes, and whether we could count them as aiming to fulfil any of the four roles we have outlined here. For instance, the Finnish code states that the aim of these guidelines 'is to support the responsible use of freedom of speech in mass communication and encourage discourse on professional ethics'. It was not clear to us whether the discourse they wish to encourage is supposed to include the public, and so whether we should count the code as one that intends to perform a public-facing function. Accordingly, we have employed a 'safety-first' approach. Where there was significant opacity about whether a code took itself to be performing one of our four roles we have counted it as not aiming to perform it.[27]

We found that every one of the codes set out to guide the actions of journalists by offering normative guidance. As explained above, this is the most common function that codes play and, indeed, it is often assumed to be the only one. A comfortable majority of the codes – nine of fourteen – also cited the possibility of some form of disciplinary action arising from violation of the principles they laid out. This is also to be expected. While different countries adopt different approaches to regulation, and the ideal of *self-regulation* (as opposed to state regulation) is highly prized, it is generally accepted that some disciplinary measures should be enacted to prevent the emergence of an effective free-for-all.

What was surprising was the scarcity of codes directly addressing the public at large and stating that this was a document intended to be of use to them. In fact, only four of the codes, less than a third, identified this clearly as an aim. It may be that this was an unstated assumption, and as evidence of that we may point out that the codes were freely available on the internet. It is also important to note that the press councils themselves generally claim to have a public-facing role. All the same, it is significant that this would not be obvious to anyone who was only reading the code.

Perhaps our most striking finding, though, was that no code explicitly committed to playing an identity-forming role. The language used in the French and Swiss codes could be interpreted as leaning in that direction,[28] and the Swedish code does state that it is 'intended to provide support' for a 'responsible attitude', but in line with our 'safety-first' principle, this was not sufficient to count as a commitment to playing this role. The preambles and forewords to the codes did set out some lofty aspirations, and an argument could perhaps be made that this also gestures in the direction of an ethical identity. Again, we do not view this as sufficient to demonstrate an intention to play the part of an identity-forming code. It does not appear that many press codes are trying to play the unifying role of a Hippocratic Oath.

We believe that this presents something of a gap in the market. In particular, this is an opportunity that should be seized in the UK, where public trust in the press remains critically low.[29] As the introduction to the Leveson Report (2012: 3) notes, it was the seventh time in 70 years that the UK government felt compelled by concerns about the conduct of the press to commission such a report. How codes may be written to assist in forging more robust professional identities is an open question and one that could be a fruitful avenue for future research. One possibility is to build on the idea we discussed earlier that codes could provide the foundation for a 'shield-wall' where strength comes from the collective structure rather than the efforts of a single individual. This may, for instance, involve emphasising solidarity as a value endorsed in the code, stressing obligations that journalists have to each other, as well as to the public, and ensuring that codes are constructed in a more 'bottom-up' way.

Conclusions

In line with our methodological approach of using philosophical thinking to clarify and respond to real-world problems, there are three main points to take away. First, codes should state unambiguously and succinctly what they are for. Ideally, this should be in the preamble or in a dedicated section towards the front of the code. Although the function of a code may seem obvious, one of the points we hope to have shown in this paper is that there are, in fact, a range of functions that codes might serve. Being explicit will ensure that those writing the code are better able to see the pitfalls we discussed above – and avoid

Carl Fox

Joe Saunders

John Steel

Julie Firmstone

Charlotte Elliott-Harvey

Martin Conboy

Jane Mulderrig

them. By making it clear what the code is actually meant to do, it will also illuminate what it is not meant to do, which will help to manage the expectations of practitioners and the public.

Second, the dearth of public-facing codes suggests that press councils across Europe could be doing a much better job of communicating their standards to the public. We believe that it should be considered good practice to explicitly state this as an aim in the opening section of a press code of ethics. Relatedly, press councils who do not already invite the public to take an active part in writing and reviewing codes[30] are passing up an opportunity to include citizens in the broader conversation about what press standards should be. Eliciting their assistance in writing codes is, of course, just one way in which this goal could be advanced, but it would be an important start.

Finally, there is considerable scope for press codes of ethics to be more ambitious. In general, this would entail trying to perform functions above and beyond the standard ones of offering advice and underpinning disciplinary procedures. More specifically, press councils should be open to the idea of using their codes of ethics as the basis for redeveloping and strengthening a rich and reason-giving professional identity. Alongside the ways in which this might buttress ethical behaviour, it is worth exploring because journalism can make an enormous contribution to the flourishing of a democratic society. When done right, it should be a source of pride and meaning for practitioners.

It is important not to overstate the case for codes of ethics as a tool for directly raising ethical standards in the press. Clearly there are other factors that are more significant in driving the conduct of journalists and other media actors. In this paper we have, however, tried to show that it is a mistake to dismiss codes of ethics out of hand and offered some suggestions for making better use of them.

Declaration

The research for this paper was funded by the AHRC. Project reference: AH/R00644X/1. The authors would like to thank the AHRC for their generous support.

Notes

[1] In a similar vein, Davis (1991: 150) notes that codes are described as 'self-serving, unrealistic, inconsistent, mere guides for novices, too vague, or unnecessary'

[2] On this point, see also Bertrand (2017: 2): 'Paradoxically, the media are accused of every sin at a time when they have never been better. ... The media are certainly better today, but still mediocre'

[3] For additional global context see the work of the Ethical Journalism Network (https://ethicaljournalismnetwork.org), for instance the *Ethics in the news* reports and podcast series

[4] For a discussion of the relationship between the news media and a democratic system of government see Christians et al. (2009: 114-135)

⁵ See Frost (2011: 266): 'Many professions and trades have raced to introduce codes of practice … in the light of rising consumer consciousness'

⁶ The countries in our study are Austria, Belgium, Denmark, France, Finland, Germany, Ireland, the Netherlands, Norway, Slovakia, Sweden, Switzerland and the UK. For further information on this project see https://www.derby.ac.uk/departments/ humanities/defining-freedom-of-the-press/

⁷ Such as regulatory context, the commercial environment and the broader press culture within each country included in the study

⁸ For a discussion of some of our findings with respect to the particular case of local journalism see Firmstone et al. (2022)

⁹ For some non-descriptive treatments of this subject, see Slattery (2014), Herrscher (2002) and Christians (1985)

10 Pursuing this thought further, it is apparent that the divisions between various branches of ethics and, indeed, philosophy more generally, are somewhat artificial. There are often ideas from other philosophical disciplines that ethicists pick up and use in their work. For instance, recent work in applied ethics and political philosophy on racism and sexism owes a great deal to insights gleaned from social metaphysics and to epistemology. See, for instance, the influence of Haslanger (2000) and Fricker (2007)

¹¹ Chadwick (2009) makes a similar point without rejecting the terminology of 'applied ethics' and argues instead for greater interdisciplinarity as standard practice

¹² On this point, see also Sanders (2003), Christians et al. (2009), Christians (2011) and Christians (2019)

¹³ See https://rsf.org/en/ranking/2018. Although these measures are imperfect and 'an ongoing evaluation of these scores is necessary' (Martin et al. 2016: 106), we suggest that they offer a useful starting point for more focused studies

¹⁴ There are two codes of ethics for the Dutch and French-speaking Belgian press, overseen by the Council for Journalism and the Council for Ethical Journalism respectively

¹⁵ See, for instance, Schwartz (2001: 248)

¹⁶ For alternative perspectives on the various kinds of contributions that codes can play see Schwartz (2001), Frankel (1989) and Beyerstein (1993)

¹⁷ For an account of the potential significance of the Helsinki Declaration for other professions see Lawlor and Morley (2017). For discussion on these and related points, the authors are grateful to Rob Lawlor, Helen Morley and Kevin Macnish

¹⁸ Writing in the medical context, Beauchamp and Childress claim that 'codes tend to foster and reinforce member-identification with and institutional conformity to the prevailing values of the profession' (1994: 7)

¹⁹ For an illuminating discussion of shame see Nussbaum (2004: 211) who makes a crucial distinction between what she calls constructive shame and primitive shame. While the latter is irrational and corrosive, constructive shame can be warranted and a potent motivation to engage in remedial action. Constructive shame is only possible when it is tied to suitably justified moral principles. Although we do not have space to explore this idea here, a code of ethics could provide the right kind of reference point to anchor constructive shame for journalists

20 How we perceive ourselves, and how we think that others perceive us, can make a tangible difference to our behaviour. Miller (2018: 174-177) points to studies showing that labelling participants as virtuous actually led them to behave in more virtuous ways

²¹ The French press council – the Conseil de Déontologie Journalistique et de Mediation (CDJM) – does not have its own code of ethics but, instead, relies on three 'foundational' texts (https://cdjm-org.translate.goog/les-chartes/?_x_tr_sl=fr&_x_tr_ tl=en&_x_tr_hl=en&_x_tr_pto=sc). The first of which (listed first on their website) is the National Syndicate of Journalists' code of ethics. As this is the official code of the French journalists' trade union we have taken it to be the one that is likely to be the most

Carl Fox

Joe Saunders

John Steel

Julie Firmstone

Charlotte Elliott-
Harvey

Martin Conboy

Jane Mulderrig

important and influential for French journalists and so decided to focus on it for the purposes of this study

[22] Interestingly, the International Federation of Journalists chooses to use similar language in its Global Charter for Journalists, which was adopted in 2019. Several clauses use the phrases 'the journalist shall' or 'the journalist will': https://www.ifj.org/who/rules-and-policy/global-charter-of-ethics-for-journalists.html

[23] We thank an anonymous reviewer for pushing us on this point

[24] See fn. 6

[25] This applies to both versions. See fn. 8

[26] See fn.21

[27] It is, of course, perfectly possible that a code may come to play a role that its authors did not envisage for it. However, it seems to us that if press councils and other institutional actors are not pushing for it and raising awareness of it then this is significantly less likely to happen

[28] For example, both codes made assertions about what *journalists do*. One natural way to interpret those assertions is that failure to do those things would constitute a failure to be a journalist

[29] See also the Reuters Institute Digital Report 2021 which was mentioned earlier. Overall trust in the news in the UK was reported at 36 per cent, which was significantly below the global average

[30] As an example of this we can take the process used by the UK regulator IMPRESS to write the first incarnation of its code in 2016, which solicited priorities from members of the public and used workshops to develop those priorities further: see https://www.impress.press/standards/about-standards-code.html

References

Beauchamp, T. L. and Childress, J. F. (1994) *Principles of biomedical ethics*, Oxford, Oxford University Press, fourth edition

Bertrand, C.-J. (2005) Introduction: Media accountability, *Pacific Journalism Review: Te Koakoa*, Vol. 11, No. 2 pp 5-16

Bertrand, C.-J. (2017) *Media ethics and accountability systems*, Abingdon, Routledge

Beyerstein, D. (1993) The functions and limitations of professional codes of ethics, Winkler, E. and Coombs, J. R. (eds) *Applied ethics: A reader*, Oxford, Blackwell

Chadwick, R. (2009) What is 'applied' in applied ethics?, *Journal of Applied Ethics and Philosophy*, Vol. 1 pp 1-7

Christians, C. G., Glasser, T. L., McQuail, D., Nordenstreng, K. and White, R. A. (2009) *Normative theories of the media: Journalism in democratic societies*, Chicago, University of Illinois Press

Christians, C. (1985) Enforcing media codes, *Journal of Mass Media Ethics*, Vol. 1, No. 1 pp 14-21

Christians, C. (2011) The philosophy of technology: Globalization and ethical universals, *Journalism Studies*, Vol. 12, No. 6 pp 727-737

Christians, C. (2019) *Media ethics and global justice: An ontological perspective*, New York, Cambridge University Press

Cooper, T. (1990) Comparative international media ethics, *Journal of Mass Media Ethics*, Vol. 5, No. 1 pp.3-14

Cronin, M. M. and McPherson, J. B. (1995) Pronouncements and denunciations: An analysis of state press association ethics codes from the 1920s, *Journalism and Mass Communication Quarterly*, Vol. 72, No. 4 pp 890-901

Culver, K. B. (2017) Disengaged ethics: Code development and journalism's relationship with 'the public', *Journalism Practice*, Vol. 11, No. 4 pp 477-492

Davis, M. (1991) Thinking like an engineer: The place of a code of ethics in the practice of a profession, *Philosophy and Public Affairs,* Vol. 20, No. 2 pp 150-167

Firmstone, J, Steel, J., Conboy, M., Elliott-Harvey, C., Fox, C., Mulderrig, J., Saunders, J. and Wragg, P. (2022) Trust and ethics in local journalism: A distinctive orientation towards responsible journalism and ethical practices, Lynch, J. and Rice, C. (eds) *Responsible journalism in conflicted societies: Trust and public service across new and old divides*, London, Routledge

Frankel, M. S. (1989) Professional codes: Why, how, and with what impact?, *Journal of Business Ethics*, Vol. 8 pp 109-115

Frost, C. (2011) *Journalism ethics and regulation*, Harlow: Longman, Pearson, third edition

Fricker, M. (2007) *Epistemic injustice: Power and the ethics of knowing*, Oxford, Oxford University Press

Hafez, K. (2002) Journalism ethics revisited: A comparison of ethics codes in Europe, North Africa, the Middle East, and Muslim Asia, *Political Communication,* Vol. 19, No. 2 pp 225-250

Hale, B. (2011) The methods of applied philosophy and the tools of the policy sciences, *International Journal of Applied Philosophy,* Vol. 25, No. 2 pp 215-232

Harcup, T. (2020) *What's the point of news? A study in ethical journalism*, Basingstoke, Palgrave Macmillan

Haslanger, S. (2000) Gender and race: (What) are they? (What) do we want them to be?, *Nous,* Vol. 34, No. 1 pp 31-55

Herrscher, R. (2002) A universal code of journalism ethics: Problems, limitations, and proposals, *Journal of Mass Media Ethics,* Vol. 17, No. 4 pp.277-289

Himelboim, I. and Limor, Y. (2008) Media perception of freedom of the press: A comparative international analysis of 242 codes of ethics, *Journalism,* Vol. 9, No. 3 pp 235-265

Laitila, T. (1995) Journalistic codes of ethics in Europe, *European Journal of Communication,* Vol. 10, No. 4 pp 527-544

Lawlor, R. and Morley, H. (2017) Climate change and professional responsibility: A declaration of Helsinki for engineers, *Science and Engineering Ethics,* Vol. 23, No. 5 pp 1431-1452

Leveson, B. H. (2012) *An inquiry into the culture, practices and ethics of the press: Executive summary and recommendations*, London, The Stationery Office. Available online at https://assets.publishing.service.gov.uk/government/uploads/system/uploads/attachment_data/file/229039/0779.pdf, accessed on 7 April 2021

Limor, Y. and Himelboim, I. (2006) Journalism and moonlighting: An international comparison of 242 codes of ethics, *Journal of Mass Media Ethics,* Vol. 21, No. 4 pp 265-285

Martin, J. D., Abbas, D. and Martins, R. J. (2016) The validity of global press ratings: Freedom House and Reporters Sans Frontières, 2002-2014, *Journalism Practice,* Vol. 10, No. 1 pp 93-108

Miller, C. B. (2018) *The character gap: How good are we?*, Oxford, Oxford University Press

Newman, N., Fletcher, R., Schulz, A., Simge, A., Robertson, C. T. and Kleis Nielsen, R. (2021) *Reuters Institute digital news report 2021*, Oxford, Reuters Institute for the Study of Journalism, tenth edition. Available online at https://reutersinstitute.politics.ox.ac.uk/sites/default/files/2021-06/Digital_News_Report_2021_FINAL.pdf, accessed on 6 January 2022

Nussbaum, M. (2004) *Hiding from humanity: Disgust, shame, and the law*, Princeton, NJ, Princeton University Press

Roberts, C. (2012) Identifying and defining values in media codes of ethics, *Journal of Mass Media Ethics,* Vol. 27, No. 2 pp 115-129

Sanders, K. (2003) *Ethics & journalism*, London, SAGE

Carl Fox

Joe Saunders

John Steel

Julie Firmstone

Charlotte Elliott-Harvey

Martin Conboy

Jane Mulderrig

Schwartz, M. (2001) The nature of the relationship between corporate codes of ethics and behaviour, *Journal of Business Ethics*, Vol. 32 pp 247-262

Slattery, K. L. (2014) Ethics and journalism standards: An examination of the relationship between journalism codes of ethics and deontological moral theory, Wyatt, W. N. (ed.) *The ethics of journalism: Individual, institutional and cultural influences*, London, I. B. Tauris and the Reuters Institute for the Study of Journalism pp 33-53

Ward, S. J. A. (2010) *Global journalism ethics.* Montreal and Kingston, McGill-Queen's University Press

Ward, S. J. A. (2015) *The invention of journalism ethics: The path to objectivity and beyond*, Montreal and Kingston, McGill-Queen's University Press, second edition

Wilkins, L. and Brennan, B. (2004) Conflicted interests, contested terrain: Journalism ethics codes then and now, *Journalism Studies*, Vol. 5, No. 3 pp 297-309

Wolff, J. (2020) *Ethics and public policy: A philosophical inquiry*, London, Routledge second edition

Notes on the contributors

Dr Carl Fox, Lecturer, Inter-Disciplinary Ethics Applied (IDEA) Centre, University of Leeds

Joe Saunders, Assistant Professor, Department of Philosophy, Durham University

John Steel, Professor of Journalism, College of Arts, Humanities and Education, University of Derby

Julie Firmstone, Associate Professor, School of Media and Communication, University of Leeds

Charlotte Elliott-Harvey, Honorary Research Fellow, Department of Journalism Studies, University of Sheffield

Martin Conboy, Professor, Department of Journalism Studies, University of Sheffield

Jane Mulderrig, Senior Lecturer, School of English, University of Sheffield

Chrisanthi Giotis

Missing what counts. Can Google and Facebook be forced to support quality news?

Australia's News Media Bargaining Code (NMBC) is often referred to as a world first in attempting to force digital platforms to pay for news products. The justification for this legislation is the safeguarding of public interest journalism which is often expensive to create and does not attract the same attention, especially online, as some other forms of popular journalism. Therefore, it is odd that there is no attempt also to safeguard the quality of that public interest journalism – especially when the reviews leading up to the legislation specifically acknowledge that poor quality public interest journalism is possible. One explanation for this omission is the fact that the NMBC has emerged from Australia's competition regulator and is, therefore, concerned with monetary exchange; currently, there is no way of accounting for the extra value provided by high quality public interest journalism. This paper explores the possibility of applying social accounting metrics to quality journalism. The logistical difficulties, dangers and opportunities that emerge through this exploration reveal the importance of journalism scholarship taking part in wider debates about how cultural life and citizenship are valued, particularly post Covid-19.

Key words: public interest journalism, social accounting metrics, Australia's News Media Bargaining Code

Introduction: The quality blind spot

Australia's News Media Bargaining Code (NMBC) is lauded as the world's first legislation forcing digital platforms to pay for news and which both the UK and Canada are looking at seriously. It embodies a societal understanding and acceptance that a strong information ecosystem requires economically healthy news businesses, producing diverse news offerings on topics of public significance. The legislation is derived from three convictions: first, that digital platforms have created

Chrisanthi Giotis an uneven playing field when it comes to the money-making aspects of the distribution of news; second, that this bargaining imbalance must be rectified; and third, that platforms must do more to support news businesses. Although the legislation is not enacted by the government, the threat of the legislation has forced Google and Facebook to make better deals with news businesses whose content they carry (Hannam 2022). The creation of the legislation also reveals much about the way news is valued by society – and the ways in which it is not. The issue of safeguarding quality is not embraced by the Australian Competition and Consumer Commission ACCC (Giotis, Molitorisz and Wilding 2023) even though its own report acknowledges that poor-quality public interest journalism is possible (ACCC 2019: 287).

The question here is this: under what circumstances could we value quality journalism in future iterations of such laws? The NMBC emerged from Australia's competition regulator and is, therefore, concerned with monetary exchange; currently there is no way of accounting for the extra value provided by high quality public interest journalism compared to poor quality public journalism. This paper explores the implications of this quality blind spot in the context of the burgeoning field of social metrics. It asks if it is possible and desirable to adopt social accounting methods to measure quality journalism. The neoliberal assumptions, logistical difficulties, dangers and opportunities that emerge through this exploration reveal the importance of journalism scholarship taking part in wider debates about how cultural life and citizenship is valued, particularly post Covid-19.

The Australian context and crisis as revelation

The Australian Competition and Consumer Commission (ACCC) began its inquiry into digital platform providers with the aim, as discussed by chairman Rod Sims, to 'fully understand the influence on Australia' of digital platform providers, especially Google and Facebook (ACCC 2017). Australia has a relatively small but culturally diverse population of about 26 million across a large continent. Australians are not avid consumers of news: with a 'news interest' rating of 51 per cent in the *Reuters Institute Digital News Report 2021*, Australia is below the 24-market average of 58 per cent; moreover, interest in news has declined by 12 percentage points throughout the past five years (Newman et al. 2021: 13). And choice is limited. In terms of pluralism and ownership, Australia has one of the world's most concentrated media markets (Dwyer, Wilding and Koskie 2021).

The ACCC concluded that public interest journalism was disappearing from the Australian landscape with reporting of judicial matters and local levels of government no longer covered with the same frequency. Having used its compulsory information gathering powers, the ACCC was able to identify – for the first time in Australia – news deserts; that is local communities left without any newspapers. It found that the net total of unique Australian local and regional newspaper titles (operating in print or online) declined by 15 per cent between 2008-2009 and 2017-2018, which translates to 106 papers. Closures during this period left 21 local government areas (LGAs) without a single local or regional newspaper. Rural and regional areas fared worse with 16 of those closures taking place in areas where the LGA did not include a city in its boundaries. In June 2019, the ACCC reports there was market failure: 'There is not yet any indication of a business model that can effectively replace the advertiser model, which has historically funded the production of [local government and local court] journalism in Australia' (ACCC 2019: 1). The government subsequently directed the ACCC to facilitate the development of a voluntary bargaining code of conduct to exist between the platforms and the news businesses so as to ensure digital platforms are redistributing some of the advertising revenues they gained, back to news businesses whose content they carried.

And then the world changed. From September 2019 to late February 2020 large areas of Australia, particularly regional Australia, were impacted by a bushfire crisis unlike any before in size and duration, starkly highlighting the importance of quality information and news provision. News outlets saw significant uplifts in digital readership as publishers brought their bushfire-related content out from behind paywalls. This was closely followed by the Covid-19 pandemic and the erosion of already scarce advertising revenue, resulting in the closure or cessation of more than 200 local and regional titles at a time when communities felt they were desperately needed.

In this environment of crisis, the ACCC's progress report to the government in April 2020 indicates that the resolution through this voluntary process of the core issue of payment for content was highly unlikely. On 20 April 2020, the government announced its intention to implement a mandatory code of conduct. There is no doubt there was an element of political theatre to this announcement with the Australian government keen to show it was doing something; however, the crisis was also a revelation of how much quality journalism provision matters after all.

This crisis-revelation phenomenon is not limited to journalism. In the context of evaluating the public benefit of arts and culture Meyrick and Barnett (2021: 75) write that 'during Covid-19, the public role of arts and culture has become self-evident. The challenge is to match this realization with a new understanding of their public value'. A parallel argument can be made in terms of journalism. The creation of the NMBC represents an acknowledgement of the importance of news businesses to democracy, and the need to protect those businesses – even to the extent of a conservative government advocating market intervention. But there is still much work to do in terms of articulating what exactly is valued, and protecting that value from ill-designed interventions which may do more harm than good.

The quality – public interest nexus

In his book *Social media and the public interest* (2019), Philip Napoli notes that the term 'public interest' has a very long, complex and contested history in the world of media and journalism. This is because 'public interest' serves as a central component of the professional and organisational missions of journalists and news organisations as well as government regulation and initiatives. What is important to note in the context of this paper's focus on social utility is that, conceptually, the public interest is not just about the much-lauded fourth estate role of journalism. Napoli draws attention to the fact that historical interpretations are characterised by broad 'notions of public service and social responsibility' (Napoli 2019: 19-20). Cha uses foundational media theory from Denis McQuail to argue public interest is:

> the complex of supposed informational, cultural, and social benefits to the wider society which go beyond the immediate, particular and individual interest of those who participate in public communication, whether as senders or receivers (McQuail cited in Cha 2020: 67).

These descriptions highlight that public interest journalism has a social dimension. But these descriptions do little to introduce the concept of quality – rather, there is an assumption that the information flowing through society enhances it. This assumption needs questioning. Partisan, inaccurate and socially divisive journalism on issues of public significance does not enhance the public sphere. In fact, one of the ways to distinguish between high and low quality journalism is by looking at its social utility.

An extensive review of literature looking at journalism quality, carried out as part of commissioned research for the Digital Platforms Inquiry (Wilding et. al. 2018), finds that content quality is discussed in journalism literature through three distinct categories, one of which is the broad social functions which news performs (see category C in the table below). In essence, the literature affirms that quality news which undertakes watchdog functions, services critical information needs, is geographically relevant and represents social diversity performs social utility functions. By implication, then, poor quality news does not perform the same socially valuable functions.

Quality indicators – content attributes

Indicator	What it indicates	Indicator	What it indicates
A. Core Standards of Practice		C. Broader Social Functions	
Accuracy	Content is factual, verified and not misleading; opinion is based on accurate information and does not omit facts; material presented in the body corresponds with the headline.	Power watchdog	Scrutinises the activities and conduct of powerful interests so they can be held democratically and socially accountable.

 Copyright 2022-1. Ethical Space: The International Journal of Communication Ethics. All rights reserved. Vol 20, No 1 2023

Clarity	Easy to understand; distinguishes fact from opinion.	Public sphere	Facilitates deliberative, rational and representative public discourse.
Fairness	Material is fairly presented; persons or groups unfavourably portrayed given right of reply.	Critical Information Needs (CINs)	Gives details of emergencies, risks, health, welfare, education, transportation, economic opportunities, environment, civic information and political information.
Privacy and protection from harm	Respects privacy; avoids causing substantial offence, distress or risk to health or safety (unless it is in the public interest).	Geographic relevance	Provides original local news voice for local communities; reports on local institutions, decision making processes and events.
Balance	Presentation of contrasting information and viewpoints from different sources.	Usefulness	Provides citizens with information they can use to make effective decisions that benefit their personal and civic lives.
Integrity and transparency	Avoids or discloses potential conflicts of interest; content has not been produced via unethical or deceptive means.	Diversity (social)	Positive coverage of minority groups; variety of content appeals to a range of social groups; multicultural references.
B. Core Professional Practice Indicators			
Immediacy	Publication and updating of breaking news as soon as practicable (after fact-checking) for each given format.	Analysis	Rational, knowledgeable and insightful interpretation of events and issues that helps people make sense of their world.
Authority	Stories use the expertise of authoritative and reliable sources; corporate or partisan sources are clearly identified.	Originality	Content is produced in-house through original research, interviews, verification of information, self-taken photos.
Depth and breadth of coverage	Explaining background context, causes and consequences involved; range of content from range of genres.	Creativity	Written and illustrated with creative flair; innovative use of technology; evinces multimedia richness (websites).
Ethical conduct in newsgathering	Uses fair, honest, responsible means to gather material.	Presentation	Uses a gratifying narrative and layered information; format is captivating, aesthetically pleasing, well-illustrated, technically and textually error-free, and easy to navigate (e.g. websites).

(Wilding et al. 2018: 86)

Indeed, the Digital Platforms Inquiry final report highlights:

> It is important to distinguish 'high quality journalism' from 'public interest journalism' ... journalism may be produced with the purpose of examining matters of public significance, meeting the definition of 'public interest journalism', without meeting minimum quality standards – for example by failing to be accurate or failing to clearly distinguish reporting from the presentation of opinion (ACCC 2019: 287).

In the quotation above, the ACCC points to issues of accuracy, fairness and clarity – all issues identified in the journalism literature (see table above – section B) as core standards of practice. This is the one quality safeguard that is written into the NMBC: for news businesses to sign up and benefit from the NMBC provisions, they must ascribe to an internal or external professional standards scheme. Putting to one side questions of the effectiveness of such standards schemes, particularly when not subject to independent oversight, such an approach takes a very narrow view of quality – ignoring the social aspects fostered by quality news summarised in table C. Such an approach is at odds with the legislation's overarching *raison d'être* to support news businesses *because of* the broad social functions they serve in democracy. However, in defence of the legislators, they are not alone in struggling to capture the broad social value of news – a similar blind spot is present in the world of media metrics.

Matt Carlson (2018: 407) argues that media organisations have struggled to describe their value to society in normative terms. He describes historical events which coalesce to see audience reach evolve as the traditional media measurement used to prove social worth; the argument is that the larger the audience, the more worth is created through the public interest journalism having a larger reach. However, such a view:

> ... narrows journalistic content to an idealized subset of hard news and leaves open all non-hard news content to accusations of being there purely to drive up profits. Such arguments reveal the normative limits of much talk about journalism and ignore the social value of a variety of news formats and topics (ibid).

These problems in the field of journalism are echoed in the NMBC legislation. In the first place, the legislation creates a similar artificial distinction between hard and soft news. The definitions contained in the code create two categories of news: 'core news' and 'covered news'. Producing core news determines whether or not a company qualifies for cover by the legislation. Core news content means content that reports, investigates or explains:

> (a) issues or events that are relevant in engaging Australians in public debate and in informing democratic decision-making; or

(b) current issues or events of public significance for Australians at a local, regional or national level.

'Covered' content is defined as 'core content' as well as content that reports, investigates or explains current issues or events of interest to Australians. The explanatory materials released with the draft legislation in July 2020 show the ACCC accepts an understanding of news business economics that includes cross-subsidy of democracy/community-enhancing news through more commercial/popular news products (ACCC 2020: 14).

But as Carlson describes above, this ignores the potential social utility of quality non-hard news items. So, for example, a movie review which includes a quality discussion of diversity issues potentially is included in category C above. Likewise, the immediate classification of all 'hard news' as worthy of support ignores the well-documented social damage which is done by poor quality news which involves race elements (Anderson 2015; Jakubowicz 2003).

The importance of somehow including quality in this equation becomes even more apparent when considering the way in which measuring changes behaviours; when newsrooms give journalists and editors access to audience metrics it impacts on editorial decisions (Petre 2015). Carlson (2018: 412) points out: 'Scholarly research into measurable journalism needs to consider how measuring alters shared imagining of what journalism is and what it is out to do.' This concern about how measuring changes behaviours and professional ethos is echoed in the literature on cultural products more broadly, with authors pointing to neoliberal biases entrenched in current cultural metrics (Phiddian et al. 2017; Meyrick and Tully 2021). Furthermore, there is the concern raised by moral philosophers that market logics corrupt actions that should be governed by other logics, such as the logic of community (Bruni 2013). These dangers are explored in more detail further on. However, on the opposite side of the coin is the argument that 'what is not measurable is often ignored' (Carlson 2018: 412). The exploration below is guided by the belief that we cannot afford to ignore the question of quality. We must, at least, consider options.

Can the value of news be measured?
Some political economy studies are powerful in articulating the value of journalism to society. For example, Gao, Lee and Murphey (2020) conducted a study of public finance outcomes for local governments which had lost their local papers. Using a multitude of control factors, they show that newspaper closures have a long-term impact on government fiscal efficiency. They find: 'Newspaper closures lead to higher borrowing costs in the long run, suggesting that alternative sources of media, such as the internet, are not acting as sufficient substitutes for these local newspapers' (ibid: 447). This study seems to shape much of the ACCC's concern in terms of identifying emerging

Chrisanthi Giotis local newspaper deserts. Another political economy study, which again looked at long-term trends, finds, in India, a strong news environment means better responses from politicians to issues of famine and hunger. Besley and Burgess (2000: 9) find those states 'that are most responsive to food production shocks also tend to be those with high levels of newspaper circulation'.

Effectively, these studies articulate the social utility of the 'power watchdog' value to society (see table C). However, these studies do not measure quality. Gao, Lee and Murphey (2020) place their research within a burgeoning area examining how the monitoring function provided by journalists improves corporate governance. Quality reporting is *implied* but not proven. As revealing as these studies are, they are limited. They look at a zero-sum equation: the existence of news media (and the reputational effects of coverage in news media) versus its absence. Nevertheless, there are clues that quality counts. Besley and Burgess (2000) find the ability of newspapers to perform the 'power watchdog' role is correlated to the extent of their circulation, which confirms the traditional argument put forward by newspapers that 'large news audiences may be considered a form of proof that the journalists are fulfilling journalism's public service role' (Carlson 2018: 407). However, Besley and Burgess (2000) make specific note of the fact that newspaper activity and circulation are not correlated to higher income states. This begs the question: why are people in some poorer communities willing to spend their more limited money on buying newspapers? It is possible quality may be a factor here – but again, that is only speculation – these studies do not measure quality directly.

These studies look at the overall media environment – not the social utility of individual news organisations – whereas the NMBC is based on supporting *individual* news organisations which qualify because of their production of 'core news'. Therefore, a measurement to apply to individual businesses is needed. Attempts to measure the social impact of specific news organisations exist, particularly in the United States where philanthropists play a bigger role in the funding of news and have specific social justice goals (Schiffrin and Zuckerman 2015; Wroth and Giller 2015). It is tempting to see these studies as relevant to the arguments in this paper. However, there is an important distinction between social impact and social utility. Measurements geared towards philanthropists focus on *social justice impacts* such as reporting on underserved communities or campaigning investigative journalism that is successful in changing policy. This is related to, but not the same, as measuring the everyday social utility of the existence of news organisations in an information ecosystem.

A study which comes closer to looking at the social utility of individual news businesses was conducted by a consultancy firm (Social Ventures Australia) for the Australian government as part of its analysis of investment in Indigenous Australian media. The federal government funds 120 Indigenous Broadcasting Services (IBS) and a Social Return on Investment (SROI) analysis was conducted on three of these, one remote IBS, one regional IBS and an urban IBS (SVA 2017).

As is argued elsewhere (Giotis, Molitorisz and Wilding 2023), the use of SROI is of particular significance in the context of the NMBC because it is an accounting methodology that attaches specific prices, as proxies, for social value generated by products. Therefore, eyeballs online (audience), would no longer be the only bargaining chip. Conceivably, a higher quality news product, seen by fewer people, could still be given extra bargaining weight than a lower quality, but more popular product, because of the extra social value the quality product creates. However, this is an argument at the level of theory. At the time of writing there is no SROI method for quantifying in dollar terms the difference between higher and lesser quality news products. Instead, in line with the social justice focus of philanthropy, it is commonly used to demonstrate a positive social impact for particular vulnerable groups with the dollar proxy calculated as value added to the community (Jackson and McManus 2019; SVA 2017). In the case of Indigenous Broadcasting Services, the analysis finds a significant return on investment for the Indigenous communities they serve with 'an average across the three broadcasters of $2.87 of social, cultural and economic value for every dollar invested' (SVA 2017: 5). The issue of quality does make a cameo appearance, noting that the urban IBS is able to provide its community access to a 'high-quality studio' and this then helps recognition of Indigenous musicians and their music (ibid: 50). The analysis further notes that the quality of the broadcast technology impacts on the rate of social returns provided to the community (ibid: 68). However, this is still a far cry from making a concerted effort to measure quality content as a factor in valuing the social impact of particular organisations.

The danger: Counting the wrong values

Before any attempts to measure quality in journalism it is worth understanding what takes place in other cultural fields. In arts, quality is specifically addressed as a factor in determining financial support from government through a tool called Culture Counts, developed by the Arts Council of England. Gilmore, Glow and Johanson (2017: 282) summarise Culture Counts as an:

> evaluation system and digital platform, [which] compiles data from standardised evaluation surveys of different stakeholder groups – organisations, audiences, critics, funders and peers – and provides the means to compare and triangulate data in an accessible format. As a result, it claims to provide a more effective, democratic tool for quality measurement of art, which demonstrates the public value of funding.

The problem with this system, according to the authors, is that it replicates existing inequalities and frameworks of understanding in the arts field. That the use 'of standard post-event survey methodology

Chrisanthi Giotis … draws the publics into the same value frameworks as the other stakeholders…[and] neglects the interests of potential audiences rather than existing ones' (ibid: 291). By replicating existing frameworks defining public value this then 'works to reinforce art forms which are already prioritised by funding' (ibid: 292). A similar problem is in the evaluation of the Indigenous Broadcast Service. The SROI analysis, in the pursuit of creating dollar proxies, replicates the value-logic of economies of scale. As noted by report authors Social Ventures Australia: 'The size of an IBS's listener base is a key driver of value' (SVA 2017: 69). However, this is an imperfect understanding of social value; they go on to note (SVA 2017: 70):

> … the size of the population can challenge an IBS's ability to have deeper engagement with the community … resulting in less value per listener … [IBSs] in smaller communities can respond to emerging needs with targeted solutions, and are able to attract a higher percentage of their population as listeners.

In other words, measured on a per-person basis, the social value of small organisations is higher. However, when this value is broken down into a dollar proxy, it shifts value towards an economic rather than social logic. This replicates existing inequalities between small and large organisations with large ones able to post a higher SROI value.

The way in which market-based mechanisms distort values towards economic logic is seen, too, in the News Media Bargaining Code where a minimum turnover threshold of AU$150,000 is imposed on news businesses before they are covered by the legislation. No doubt this is because of the logic that a certain scale is needed before digital platforms start to derive benefit from the existence of an individual news platform. However, this is not necessarily conducive to supporting the overall health of the information ecosystem. As is noted in the literature (Wilding, Giotis and Koskie 2020) and acknowledged in government reports, smaller news organisations have their own unique and important role to play (ACMA 2020). Meyrick and Barnett (2021: 79) list several methods of evaluating cultural products, including SROI, which they argue all suffer from a monistic bias based in neoliberal economics 'excising a range of factors pertinent to consideration of the common good'. They also argue that there is a danger in investing in evaluative methods only to have goalposts shifted by 'governments when expedient for them to do so' (2021: 85). Accounting theorist Glen Lehman writes that early models of social accounting do not engage deeply enough with ideological assumptions and, thus, instead of acting as a critique of market forces, slide 'unconsciously back to pragmatic managerialism' (Lehman 2010: 731). However, Lehman argues that these early mistakes are fixable, and social accounting could contribute to enhancing the public sphere.

The opportunity: Capturing *zeitgeist*

The existence of SROI is an advantage, and in an environment where governments are forced to intervene to protect news businesses, those businesses can (perhaps should) do more to articulate their social value. Moreover, if we consider the argument that measuring changes behaviour, focusing on the measurement of social utility should, theoretically, drive up quality. There is also an argument for capturing the current *zeitgeist* which sees citizens in Australia articulate their concerns about the type of news industry they want.

As mentioned at the outset of this paper, the Digital Platforms Inquiry emerged thanks to a concern in Australia about the loss of local journalism. This concern is particularly pronounced in regional areas where the slow decline of print newspapers accelerated dramatically during the pandemic resulting in a raft of closures and contractions (Giotis 2020). However, community concern also accelerated and turned into action, resulting in new newspaper offerings receiving high levels of community support (Napier-Raman and Wilkins 2020). These independent papers promised to run less syndicated news content, aligning with the social utility understanding of geographic relevance as an indicator of quality.

As in other parts of the world, in Australia the pandemic also forced a reckoning with issues of injustice, especially racial inequality. The politics of this movement takes aim at the role of the media (Mason 2021; Thomas et al. 2020) and does not confine itself to street-level protests. Another reckoning taking place at this time is with Australia's media ownership concentration and, in particular, the influence of the Rupert Murdoch-owned NewsCorp. Two former prime ministers spearheaded a record-breaking Australian electoral petition of half a million signatures forcing a Senate inquiry into the issue (Samios 2020). Arguments around the Senate inquiry highlight the issue of hyper-partisanship and the fear of polarisation (Muller 2021). However, this is only one part of the puzzle, with racial justice advocates arguing that 'the concentration of media ownership, in particular by NewsCorp, perpetuates racism in Australian society' (ATN 2020).

Taken together, these developments represent a clear call by the community to take seriously the social role of news in fostering diversity and an understanding that the opposite of social utility occurs when quality is compromised by partisan media. In the journalism literature, impartiality is not usually considered an issue of social utility but rather an issue of professional standards (see table above). Indeed, impartial journalism did not develop from an ethical imperative but rather from a market logic of increasing the readership base by not alienating potential customers through strong opinions (Carlson 2018: 407). While commercial imperatives drove the uptake of impartiality, as the profession developed and codified ethics, issues of fairness in reportage were included in these documents. Moreover, these public interventions in the media market show that, in an increasingly

Chrisanthi Giotis polarised political environment, audiences want journalists to 'double-down' on impartiality and are redefining its importance in relation not only to an abstract idea of professional ethics but to the concrete role of journalism's social utility.

Of course, the question remains: is this intervention too late? Social media news distribution changes the market logic of news, the algorithms working off and rewarding emotion and because of this, online, partisan news is now more valuable in terms of audience reach. The ACCC makes special reference to this problem in its Digital Platforms Inquiry final report. It notes discussions with journalists and editors revealing how much the algorithmic preferences, and access to real-time data about how individual stories perform, are influencing their decisions about what sort of journalism to produce.

> Stakeholders participating in the ACCC's Journalists Forum held on 15 August 2018 noted that, while journalists may have always aimed to produce popular content, they now optimise for audience and algorithm behaviour with unprecedented amounts of information, in great detail, and in real-time. ... This point was reiterated by participants in the ACCC Future of Journalism Roundtable on 15 March 2019. ... As engagement and 'sharing' behaviour is determined by any kind of strong audience interaction with the content – including negative responses – this creates and compounds commercial incentives for the production of more sensationalised reporting, such as 'click-bait' or 'outrage journalism' (ACCC 2019: 343).

This market imperative creates a situation where, in modern journalism, it is hard to distinguish clearly between opinion and factual news reports. Often, there is a partisan presentation of news of public significance which mixes hyperbole and misleading information with correct and important information. One former member of the Australian Press Council argues that the problem of regulating 'fairness and balance' has reached a point where, rather than relying on complaints about a specific article, 'patterns of articles' must be considered (Podger 2021).

Market logic should never replace the professional ethic of impartiality but, in a situation where that professional standard is under increasing pressure due to market dynamics, a social metrics approach could act as a second line of defence through shifting market dynamics. A quality-evaluation approach, looking at patterns of news organisation behaviour, rather than seeking to reprimand individual instances of transgression, is in keeping with a social utility understanding of quality news. It potentially creates a positive incentive for quality impartial news if it is tied to SROI metrics for working out a news organisation's 'value'. For example, recruiting panels of citizens to look at a representative sample of articles and judge the quality of those articles could take into account a variety of metrics prized for their social utility. Accordingly, a news organisation with a pattern of higher quality articles would contribute more social utility and score a higher dollar-proxy in terms of return on investment. This sort of approach aligns with postmodern accounting theory which argues that social audits can draw citizens into public sphere discussions, transferring power and creating an information mechanism to highlight the impact of decisions on different segments of the population, while focusing on commonalities (Lehman 2010).

The panel approach hypothesised here is just one potential solution to how SROI metrics work – and we are just at the beginning of this conversation in news circles. However, there are lessons to draw from other fields. To stay with this hypothetical example of panels for a moment longer, it is important in this scenario to keep in mind that local citizens, not just consumers of the news products, should make up the panels because this then draws in 'potential audiences' who, it is argued, are locked out of the current quality evaluation of cultural products (Gilmore, Glow and Johanson 2017: 291).

Conclusion

The Digital Platforms Inquiry and the subsequent News Media Bargaining Code are a significant achievement for Australia's competition regulator. The code is credited with prompting deals worth AU$200m. (Hannam 2022). However, as with any market intervention unintended distortion is possible.

In yet another Senate inquiry into regional news, an inquiry still underway at the time of writing, a red flag is raised by an independent regional publisher who criticised the deals struck with Google and Facebook as not suitable for small publishers because of the requirement to upload six stories a day. *Cape York Weekly* editor and publisher Matt Nicholls writes of 'mastheads uploading press release material and generic content that would never see the light of day in their print publication. There is no doubt this is to appease Google's quota'.[1] To avoid this danger, the deals struck between publishers and news organisations must require design around quality news performing social utility functions.

Of course, 'the notion of defining and measuring quality in journalism is both complex and contentious' (Napoli et al. 2017: 382) and in an environment of crisis, where pure survival is at stake, asking news organisations to invest time and money in complex and unproven social utility metrics is pie in the sky thinking. Furthermore, there is no guarantee that a social utility metric can be designed in a way that does not replicate existing market inequalities. As discussed above, large news businesses are able to reach more people and thus have a higher dollar proxy even if the social utility per person is less. Larger organisations are also more able to invest in developing metrics that speak to business and government priorities.

Copyright 2023-1. Ethical Space: The International Journal of Communication Ethics. All rights reserved. Vol 20, No 1 2023   **55**

Chrisanthi Giotis It also is noted that having avoided the 'big stick' of legislation enacted, platforms are now making direct investments in news businesses. The Facebook Australian News Fund began in 2022 with AU$5m. direct investment in 54 news organisations and independent journalists across Australia, with the promise of a total of $15m. throughout three years (Walkley News 2022). The money is split, with half the funds going to newsroom sustainability and half going into projects aimed at producing public interest journalism. The decision on funding is made by judges drawn from Australia's Walkley Foundation which administers the top awards for quality journalism. Potentially, this sort of targeted investment is a better way of supporting quality journalism. But it is also worth remembering that this is a moment of corporate social responsibility coming hard on the heels of the threat of government intervention. There is no guarantee this moment will last.

In 2019, the Digital Platforms Inquiry found 21 local government areas without a single local or regional newspaper. Since then, the Public Interest Journalism Initiative's Australian Newsroom Mapping Project documents that 33 local government areas, or 6 per cent of Australia's total municipalities, are now without a local print or digital news outlet (Walkley News 2022). These findings in Australia are no surprise given the longstanding trends of news deserts that are well documented in the United States and Canada (Abernathy 2018; Public Policy Forum 2017). Covid-19 accelerated the problems in the news industry; it did not create them. There are underlying structural issues with current news businesses which have weakened the news industry for years. New structures are needed to replace the crumbling structures of the past. This paper posits that attaching a dollar proxy to the social utility of news is one of the structures of the future. At the very least it is time for journalism academics to join the conversation around cultural products and social metrics. As discussed by Meyrick and Barnett (2020: 86) 'reconstructing the category of public value is an exercise in long-overdue interdisciplinary collaboration' and journalism must play its part. But most importantly, this paper draws attention to that which is sidelined in the development of the News Media Bargaining Code, namely: quality in news needs taking into account – in every instance – whatever the measure.

Note

[1] Submission 12 available online at https://www.aph.gov.au/Parliamentary_Business/Committees/House/Communications/Regionalnewspapers/Submissions

References

Abernathy, Penelope Muse (2018) *The expanding news desert*, Center for Innovation and Sustainability in Local Media, School of Media and Journalism, University of North Carolina

ACCC (2017) ACCC commences inquiry into digital platforms. Available online at https://www.accc.gov.au/media-release/accc-commences-inquiry-into-digital-platforms

ACCC (2019) *Digital Platforms Inquiry: Final report*. Available online at https://www.accc.gov.au/system/files/Digital%20platforms%20inquiry%20-%20final%20report.pdf

ACCC (2020) Treasury Laws Amendment (News Media and Digital Platforms Mandatory Bargaining Code) Bill 2020 – Exposure Draft Explanatory Materials. Available online at https://www.accc.gov.au/system/files/Exposure%20Draft%20EM%20-%20 NEWS%20MEDIA%20AND%20DIGITAL%20PLATFORMS%20MANDATORY%20 BARGAINING%20CODE%20BILL%202020.pdf

ACMA (2020) *News in Australia: Diversity and localism, news measurement framework*, Australian Communications and Media Authority, Commonwealth of Australia. Available online at https://www.acma.gov.au/sites/default/files/2020-12/News%20 in%20Australia_Diversity%20and%20localism_News%20measurement%20 framework_1.pdf

Anderson, Leticia (2015) Countering Islamophobic media representations: The potential role of peace journalism, *Global Media and Communication*, Vol. 11 pp 255-270

ATN (2020) The concentration of media ownership in Australia is a racial justice issue, All Together Now. Available online at https://docs.google.com/forms/d/e/1FAIpQLSd0 F5rUVhTV2wPa5dijvRmDs6P5985vH3E9516Th5jGOXRATw/viewform, accessed on 12 December 2020

Besley, Timothy and Burgess, Robin (2000) Land reform, poverty reduction, and growth: Evidence from India, *The Quarterly Journal of Economics*, Vol. 115 pp 389-430

Bruni, Luigino (2013) Michael Sandel: What money can't buy: The moral limits of markets, *International Review of Economics*, Vol. 60 pp 101-106

Carlson, Matt (2018) Confronting measurable journalism, *Digital Journalism*, Vol. 6 pp 406-417

Cha, Jiyoung (2020) Crowdfunded journalism and social entrepreneurship: An examination of narrative and entrepreneur legitimacy, *Nordic Journal of Media Management*, Vol. 1 pp 63-80

Dwyer, Tim, Wilding, Derek and Koskie, Tim (2021) Australia: Media concentration and deteriorating conditions for investigative journalism, Trappel, J. and Tomaz, T. (eds) *The media for democracy monitor 2021: How leading news media survive digital transformation*, Nordicom, University of Gothenburg pp 59-94

Gao, Pengjie, Lee, Chang and Murphey, Dermot (2020) Financing dies in darkness? The impact of newspaper closures on public finance, *Journal of Financial Economics*, Vol. 135 pp 445-467

Gilmore, Abigail, Glow, Hilary and Johanson, Katya (2017) Accounting for quality: Arts evaluation, public value and the case of 'Culture counts', *Cultural Trends*, Vol. 26 pp 282-294

Giotis, Chrisanthi, Molitorisz, Sacha and Wilding, Derek (2023) How Australia's competition regulator is supporting news, but not quality, Lawrence, Regina and Napoli, Philip M (eds) *News quality in the digital age*, New York, Routledge

Giotis, Chrisanthi (2020) Digital-only local newspapers will struggle to serve the communities that need them most, *The Conversation,* 29 May. Available online at https://theconversation.com/digital-only-local-newspapers-will-struggle-to-serve-the-communities-that-need-them-most-139649, accessed on 24 June 2022

Hannam, Peter (2022) Reining in the digital giants: Rod Sims on the trials and triumphs of a decade as head of the consumer watchdog, *Guardian,* 26 February. Available online at https://www.theguardian.com/australia-news/2022/feb/26/reining-in-the-digital-giants-rod-sims-on-the-trials-and-triumphs-of-a-decade-as-head-of-the-consumer-watchdog

Jackson, Andrew and McManus, Richard (2019) SROI in the art gallery: Valuing social impact, *Cultural Trends*, Vol. 28 pp 132-145

Jakubowicz, Andrew (2003) Review: In this issue: Race for the headlines: Racism and media discourse, *Media International Australia*, Vol. 109 pp 180-183

Lehman, Glen (2010) Perspectives on accounting, commonalities and the public sphere, *Critical Perspectives on Accounting*, Vol. 21 pp 724-738

Chrisanthi Giotis

Mason, Bonita (2021) Australia's news media play an important role reminding the country that Black lives still matter, *The Conversation*, 3 June. Available online at https://theconversation.com/australias-news-media-play-an-important-role-reminding-the-country-that-black-lives-still-matter-161412

Meyrick, Julian, and Barnett, Tully (2021) From public good to public value: Arts and culture in a time of crisis, *Cultural Trends*, Vol. 30 pp 75-90

Muller, Denis (2021) Is Sky News shifting Australian politics to the right? Not yet, but there is cause for alarm, *The Conversation*, 22 February. Available online at https://theconversation.com/is-sky-news-shifting-australian-politics-to-the-right-not-yet-but-there-is-cause-for-alarm-155356

Napier-Raman, Kishor and Wilkins, Georgia (2020) Filling the void: The new wave fighting to keep regional media alive, *Crikey*, 20 May. Available online at https://www.crikey.com.au/2020/05/20/regional-newspaper-closures-community-response/

Napoli, Philip (2019) *Social media and the public interest: Media regulation in the disinformation age*, New York, Columbia University Press

Napoli, Philip M., Stonbely, Sarah, McCollough Kathleen and Renninger, Bryce (2017) Local journalism and the information needs of local communities: Toward a scalable assessment approach, *Journalism Practice*, Vol. 11 pp 373-395

Newman, Nic, Fletcher, Richard, Schulz, Anne, Simge, Andı, Robertson, Craig T. and Kleis Nielsen, Rasmus (2021) *Reuters Institute digital news report 2021*, Reuters Institute for the Study of Journalism, Oxford. Available online at https://reutersinstitute.politics.ox.ac.uk/digital-news-report/2021

Phiddian, Robert, Meyrick, Julian, Barnett, Tully and Maltby, Richard (2017) Counting culture to death: an Australian perspective on culture counts and quality metrics, *Culture Counts*, Vol. 26 pp 174-180

Petre, Caitlin (2015) *The traffic factories: Metrics at Chartbeat, Gawker Media, and The New York Times*, Tow Center for Digital Journalism, Columbia University

Podger, Andrew (2021) Forget calls for a royal commission into Australia's big media players – this is the inquiry we really need, *The Conversation*, 5 December. Available online at https://theconversation.com/forget-calls-for-a-royal-commission-into-australias-big-media-players-this-is-the-inquiry-we-really-need-171842

Public Policy Forum (2017) *The shattered mirror: News, democracy and trust in the digital age*, Ottawa, Public Policy Forum

Samios, Zoe (2020) Senate to launch media diversity inquiry after Kevin Rudd petition, *Sydney Morning Herald*, 11 November. Available online at https://www.smh.com.au/politics/federal/senate-to-launch-media-diversity-inquiry-after-kevin-rudd-petition-20201111-p56dpc.html

Schiffrin, Anya and Zuckerman, Ethan (2015) Can we measure media impact? Surveying the field, *Stanford Social Innovation Review*, Vol. 13 pp 48-51

SVA (2017) More than radio – a community asset: Social Return on Investment analyses of Indigenous Broadcasting Services, Sydney, Social Ventures Australia Consulting

Thomas, Archie, Jacubowicz, Andrew, Payne, Anne Maree and Norman, Heidi (2020) The Black Lives Matter movement has provoked a cultural reckoning about how Black stories are told, *The Conversation*, 11 November. Available online at https://theconversation.com/the-black-lives-matter-movement-has-provoked-a-cultural-reckoning-about-how-black-stories-are-told-149544

Walkley News (2022) The Walkley Foundation and Meta reveal 54 recipients in $15m funding program's first round. Available online at https://www.walkleys.com/the-walkley-foundation-and-meta-reveal-54-recipients-in-15m-funding-programs-first-round/?mc_cid=608962db53&mc_eid=c1957be395, accessed on 1 April 2022

Wilding, Derek, Fray, Peter, Molitorisz, Sacha and McKewon, Elaine (2018) *The impact of digital platforms on news and journalistic content*, Centre for Media Transition, University of Technology Sydney. Available online at https://www.accc.gov.au/system/files/ACCC+commissioned+report+-+The+impact+of+digital+platforms+on+news+and+journalistic+content,+Centre+for+Media+Transition+(2).pdf

Wilding, Derek, Giotis, Chrisanthi and Koskie, Tim (2020) *News in Australia: Diversity and localism – Review of literature and research*, Centre for Media Transition, University of Technology Sydney. Available online at https://www.acma.gov.au/sites/default/files/2020-12/News%20in%20Australia_Diversity%20and%20localism_Review%20of%20literature%20and%20research_1.pdf

Wroth, Katharine and Giller, Chip (2015) Can we measure media impact? Reading between the lines, *Stanford Social Innovation Review*, Vol. 13 pp 52-55

Note on the contributor

Chrisanthi Giotis is a lecturer in journalism at the University of South Australia and a Senior Research Fellow at the Centre for Media Transition at the University of Technology Sydney. A former journalist and deputy editor in Australia and the UK, she focuses on government, Indigenous affairs and social enterprise reporting.

Slavica Kodish

Communication and relationships in the digital age

Developments in technology over the past decade have been astounding and, as a result, the world we live in is increasingly becoming digital. We use communication technology and participate in social media platforms on a daily basis. Many of us converse with chatbots, participate in virtual simulations, or play virtual games. The popularity of cryptocurrency, microchipping, bio-hacking and digital relationships is growing. As the digital reality increases and envelops practically every aspect of human life, we are becoming increasingly dependent on technology. Technological devices are becoming our best friends and we are being shaped and molded by technology. Are genuine human relationships, conversations and dialogue possible in such a world? This paper explores the issue using as a starting point Ellul's (1964) concept of technique. Ellul believed that the objectifying power of technique that transforms everyone and everything into means was getting out of human control. What we are witnessing nowadays may even be a stage in which humans may have already lost control and accepted a value system that undermines genuine human relationships and raises questions about 21st century ethics and the future of ethics.

Key words: conversations, dialogue, digital humans, interaction, relationships

Introduction

For thousands of years, philosophers, poets, scholars, mystics and prophets have been concerned with human relationships and the state of the human condition. In the 20th and 21st centuries, this concern has significantly increased. Philosophers and scholars have been alarmed and deeply pained by the developments in the modern world. They write about alienation, a survivalist mode, disrespect, rudeness, lack of empathy, cynicism, narcissism, mistrust, nihilism, adversarial culture and dehumanisation. For example, Buber (1967) writes about the destructiveness of universal mistrust that characterises our modern age and undermines the foundation of human relationships. Fromm (1956) writes about the deterioration of the human condition in general. Arnett (1986: 3) notes the emergence of a 'Darwinian-type motif' and a survival attitude. Turkle (2012, 2015) is concerned with the lack of empathy and problematic uses of technology. Arnett and Arneson write about 'valuelessness' and 'routine cynicism' (1999). Arendt (1986) decries the fall into *making,* or a passive existence that limits human agency. Montagu and Matson (1983: xi) write about dehumanisation as one of the major evils in the modern world and portray it as 'an affliction of the spirit', a 'contagion … with wasting symptoms … and lethal effects'.

Moreover, at the beginning of 2020, a viral outbreak swept the planet and caused a public health emergency. In order to minimise the spread of the virus, various measures were taken, including social distancing, lockdowns and shelter-at-home orders. As a result, we have become more distanced from one another and more dependent on technology. Technology has had an impact on human relationships and interaction over the past several decades, but the combination of a variety of factors – the viral outbreak, measures taken to curb the viral outbreak, and the most recent and unprecedented advancements in communication technology – have had an additionally strong impact on human relationships. The world we live in is becoming increasingly digital, and projections are being made that humans will live in augmented reality worlds in the future. It is becoming more evident that technology and technological devices are slowly replacing real people and becoming our best friends. We need to ask if genuine human relationships, conversations and dialogue are possible in such a world.

In this paper, the author explores the issue using as a starting point Ellul's (1964) concept of *technique.* Technique can be understood as a more or less visible yet rather powerful, recursive and continually expanding weft that impacts various aspects of human life in a manner that Ellul considered constraining and dehumanising. Decades ago, Ellul suggested that the workings of technique in the modern world were getting out of human control. What we are witnessing nowadays may even be a stage in which the power and allure of technique are so intense that we, humans, may have already lost control and accepted the value system that characterises technique – effectiveness, efficiency, speed and a machine-like and de-spirited existence.

Methodologically, this paper follows in the tradition of interpretative communication research that focuses on meaning. The interpretative approach promotes a detailed exploration and description for the purpose of presenting a rich portrayal of an issue (see Geertz 1973). It also promotes an inclusion of lived experiences (see Eisenberg et al. 2017). The interpretative approach is logical and rational and at the same time free of excessive rationality and effectiveness, which makes it especially appropriate for an exploration of an issue with philosophical and ethical underpinnings.

The constraining weft of technique

Translating the word *technique* from French into English and other languages, for that matter, is not simple. *La technique* is typically translated into English as technical or technological. Neither of the two words fully captures the meaning of *la technique*. What adds an additional layer of difficulty when translating *la technique* into English is the high context/low context difference: French is a high-context language while English is a low-context language, and the French word *la technique* has layers of meaning that are not fully reflected in English words *technical* and *technological*. For that reason, instead of focusing on translation that might lead us to understand technique in a narrow sense, we will focus on the meaning and scope of technique.

Technique is a self-perpetuating, self-augmenting and all-encompassing system – a sort of an invisible weft or structure – that impacts societies, human behaviour, human agency and every aspect of human life. Ellul referred to technique as an *ensemble* or a *system*. A society with a technique orientation values rationality, efficiency, effectiveness, speed and progress. Ellul writes that the two most obvious characteristics of technique are rationality and artificiality. The former refers to standardisation and systematisation, while the latter refers to subjugation or even destruction of nature. The remaining five characteristics include automatism, self-augmentation, wholeness, universalism and autonomy. Automatism is about the prevalence of efficiency. Self-augmentation refers to the never-ending and augmenting nature of technique. Wholeness means that all aspects of technique share the same essence. Universalism refers to the spreading of technique worldwide. Finally, autonomy refers to the fact that technique is a closed system that has its own reality and its own laws. According to Matlock (2014), it is the characteristic of autonomy that is especially concerning because 'much of what goes on in economics, politics, philosophy, and society is dominated by technique, whether we know it or not' (par. 20).

Central values that characterise technique – rationality, efficiency and effectiveness – are all positive values. They bring order and higher levels of organisation and, in this respect, technique can be considered a positive development. The problem is that order and higher levels of organisation tend to become an end in themselves and that everything becomes subjugated to technique and its values and turned into means – humans, nature, animals and everything that exists. In short, technique objectifies everyone and everything, and everyone and everything that exists becomes a means to an end. In a technique-centred world, even the sacred and the mysterious are to become objectified. Ellul (1964) uses the example of the 'fish of the deep' to illustrate the objectifying, desacralising and demystifying power of technique:

> Technique takes possession of [the sacred] and enslaves it. The sacred cannot resist. Science penetrates to the great depths of the sea to photograph the unknown fish of the deep. Technique

captures them, hauls them up to see if they are edible – but before they arrive on deck they burst. ... Far from being restrained by any scruples before the sacred, technique constantly assails it. Everything which is not yet technique becomes so (ibid: 142).

Such a description of technique sounds bleak, harsh and fatalistic. It seems that Ellul did not envision the possibility that some and, perhaps, many individuals would admire the beauty or uniqueness of the 'fish of the deep' and return them to their natural habitat after photographing them. On the other hand, if Ellul had not used such a vivid and shocking description, we may not have paid much attention to technique and may have disregarded it as an interesting philosophical concept rather than as a matrix undermining ethical principles. In the *Humiliation of the word*, Ellul (1985) writes about the obsession with images and how images have taken centre stage and diminished the impact of language and words. In describing the 'fish of the deep' in an image creating manner, Ellul made it possible for us to understand the perils of technique unrestrained by moral considerations and inclusion of the sacred. In yet another image-creating description, Ellul shows the power of technique to diminish what it means to be human.

Ellul (1964: 6) writes: 'When technique enters into every area of life, including the human, it ceases to be external to man [sic] and becomes his very substance. It is no longer face to face with man but is integrated with him, and it progressively absorbs him.' In a 1979 interview, Ellul used the metaphors of a 'transporter' and 'vector' when referring to humans to illustrate the modifying power of technique and the dangers of a passive human existence controlled by technique (Ellul 2019). Again, we see the harsh and fatalistic tone and, again, as in the example of the 'fish of the deep', we can understand the image-creating descriptions as a device to portray the reach and power of technique. Technique's values envelop every aspect of human life to such an extent that the core of what it means to be human becomes altered.

Technique and technology

Technique sometimes gets equated with technology, and an explanation of the link between the two is in order. Technique does not refer to technology, nor is Ellul against technology and technological advancements. The confusion arises since technology and technique share many values, and it is often times difficult to distinguish between the two. Technology is based on and incorporates the values that characterise technique – rationality, effectiveness, efficiency, practicality, speed and progress. In this respect, technology and technique are similar. According to Ellul, both technique and technology are systems, and both have a modifying impact. Ellul (1980: 325) writes: 'The human being who acts and thinks today is not situated as an independent subject with respect to a technological object. He [sic] is inside the technological system, he is himself modified by the technological factor.' Furthermore, both technology and technique incorporate the principle of means to an end. Throughout history, technology has been developed to serve as a means to improve human life and advance human civilisations. Some forms of technology have also been used for destructive and untoward purposes, as we can see from numerous examples from both history and present-day events. When used for destructive and unethical purposes, technology turns humans into means to an end – just as technique does – and technology and technique become indistinguishable. Making the distinction between technology and technique has especially become difficult in modern times characterised by immense advancements in technology.

Modern-day technological advancements have amplified the values shared by both technique and technology – efficiency, effectiveness, practicality, speed and progress. Modern-day technology has additional advantages and an appeal that is practically impossible to resist.

Modern-day technology is not only practical, effective and efficient, but it also provides convenience, a sense of community and a sense of being in control. Depending on the type and purpose of a technological device, technology can also provide entertainment and fun, and spice up human lives with a sense of pleasure. The combination of the practical, efficient and effective with the convenient, entertaining, fun and pleasurable creates a special and irresistible appeal. Consequently, we become dependent on technology and allow technology to play an overly important role in our lives. We may even become subservient to technological devices. In this way, technology strengthens the technique orientation. This also means that a society with higher levels of technology is likely to have a stronger technique orientation.

Emergence of the digital world

Ellul believed that the objectifying power of technique that transforms everyone and everything into *means* was getting out of human control. Developments in technology that have made possible the emergence of the digital world suggest that humans may have lost control and that the power of technique may now be out of human control.

Over the past decade and especially over the past several years, the digital world has grown tremendously. It was fuelled by developments in communication technology and by a variety of technological advancements. The following example is illustrative of the most recent developments in the digital world and of the reality of the digital world. In March 2021, an anonymous buyer purchased a house for $500,000. This, in itself, would not be worth mentioning, if for one single reason: the house is an NFT or a non-fungible token – basically, it is a digital house that exists only in the digital sphere. The buyer is a human being, and human beings still need non-digital houses to live in, so why would a human being purchase a digital house? It turns out that purchasing a NFT is a good investment. The market for NFTs is growing, and buying NFTs in the form of digital art, digital songs, cryptocurrencies, or even a digital house is a new way of investing.

The NFT market is only one of the many recent developments that exemplify the reality of the digital world. Some other developments include microchipping and plans to connect the human brain to a computer. Microchipping refers to inserting a microchip in one's hand that then serves for opening doors, paying for public transportation, purchasing cafeteria snacks, or unlocking one's computer (see, e.g., Gillies 2017). Experiments aimed at connecting the human brain with a computer are currently underway, and success has been noted with monkeys. Even swimming has gone digital. In 2017, Speedo introduced an app for iPhone that helps swimmers reach their fitness goals (Samuely n.d.). In 2021, Speedo went a step further by announcing the Fastskin 4.0 concept as the 'most intelligent swimsuit of all time'. The swimsuit will have a built-in AI coach that will enable the swimmer to swim 4 per cent faster (Whatsnew2Day 2021).

While NFTs, microchipping, the human/computer interface and the future Fastskin 4.0 may be considered outliers and not representative of general trends, the use of smartphones, computers and other technological devices is quite common. Being active on social media and conversing with chatbots has skyrocketed. New types and variations of social media continue to emerge (see Foreman 2017). Billions of email messages are sent every day. In 2019, the number of global email users was 3.9 billion. The number is expected to grow to 4.48 billion in 2024 while the number of email messages sent daily is expected to reach 347 billion in 2023 (Statista n.d.). Texting is ubiquitous, and the volume of text messages enormous. The digital world is very much present, and all of us who use communication technology are a part of the digital world to a smaller or larger extent.

Some of us were born and grew up in a pre-Internet and pre-advanced technology world and, to us, technology may still have a primarily practical purpose. Some of us, however, grew up with tablets, smartphones and the internet, and we do not know of a world without advanced technological devices. We are sometimes referred to as digital natives and are very comfortable communicating and forming relationships in the digital world and we love the immersion in the digital world as attested by statistical data. Statistics and research show that the amount of screen time has been increasing over the years.

In 2015, tweens spent on average 4.36 hours of screen time per day while teens spent on average 6.40 hours per day. Homework and school-related work were not included in the total number of hours (Common Sense Media 2015). Data from 2019 show an increase: 4.41 hours of screen time for tweens and 7.22 hours of screen time for teens (Common Sense Media 2019). Reports of adults' use of screen time is higher because they include work-related responsibilities. In 2019, screen time for adults was on average 10.09 hours per day. In March 2020, because of the Covid-19 pandemic, it jumped to 13.28 hours per day (*Eyesafe* 2020).

Slavica Kodish

The digital world is practical and convenient. We can be in touch with our friends and family members, communicate with colleagues and business partners, and we can reach people who live far away and communicate with people from all over the world. The digital world is also empowering and enjoyable. We can create videos featuring ourselves, express our views and ideas, or describe relevant events in our lives or our family lives. Anyone who wishes can have a social media account or a number of accounts and present themselves in any manner they wish. Social media accounts can be truthful and contain accurate information and photos, or they can be 'polished' with Photoshopped images and Photoshopped videos. In some cases, the information can be misrepresented to such an extent that it is inaccurate and false. We can also create objects in what is typically referred to as augmented reality (see, e.g., Werner 2017). The digital world provides practically endless options and opportunities. Almost 70 years ago – Ellul's *Technological society* was published in France in 1954 – Ellul presciently wrote about the 'hoaxes' of technique that seemingly keep people happy and content. The digital world abounds in 'hoaxes' of all kinds and keeps us seemingly happy and content.

Communication and relationships in the digital world

The digital world provides almost endless opportunities for communicating and forming relationships. We can communicate instantly in a simple and convenient manner and we can be connected with as many people as we wish. We can also end the connection by a simple click or by un-friending someone. We can also post our thoughts, worries and concerns on social media or the internet and get likes, dislikes, bad advice, excellent advice, a thoughtful or not so thoughtful comment, or we can simply be ignored. The digital world is also changing the nature of communication and relationships.

In-person communication and interaction have been reduced and replaced to a large extent with their mediated counterparts. Use of cell phones during in-person interactions has increased and conversations are often times interrupted by cell phone ringing or by one or both interactants checking their text messages. Families tend to spend less time together and when they do, cell phones are often at a hand's reach. An interesting new development are online or digital relationships. Instead of forming a romantic relationship or a friendship in a traditional sense of the word by spending time together, some relationships are entirely digital. Various 'how to' manuals exist – naturally, in a digital format – that help those who are in a digital relationship build a relationship and avoid various digital pitfalls. For example, it is important to know that different posting styles can lead to conflict and that micro-cheating should be avoided.

Mediated communication and relationships are not without a price tag. A Pew Research Center report shows negative impact of communication devices and social media on romantic relationships (see Vogels and Anderson 2020). Friendships have also been negatively affected, and especially those that involve children (see Turkle 2015).

The 2020 pandemic

The 2020 viral outbreak significantly increased the use of communication technology and, consequently, increased the dependence on technology. All of us learned a new concept – social distancing. We also learned that gatherings of every type including family gatherings could be detrimental to health – our own and others'. Masks had to be worn at all times while outside of one's home and in some cases even while canoeing or jogging. For the greater good and in order to prevent the spread of the virus, face-to-face interaction was significantly reduced or minimised. As a result, the use of communication technology exploded. Zoom became a staple, social media became indispensable, and conversations with chatbots increased dramatically.

During the viral outbreak, technology helped us stay connected and it helped us socialise in a mediated manner. It also made it possible for us to talk to the teladoc and seek medical advice without leaving our homes, order food and necessities online, work from home and stay informed. Technology also provided solace, entertainment and comfort. An already high reliance on technology substantially increased during 2020 and 2021 and deepened the immersion in the digital world. Did the increased reliance on technology and the immersion in the digital world make us happier, and more fulfilled? Did it promote communication, and did it deepen and enrich our relationships?

Life in the digital world

Research suggests that over the past two years overall health, including emotional and mental health, has been negatively affected. It is not fully clear, however, which factors played the main role. It may have been the fear of getting ill or the consequences of contracting the virus; it could have been the pain caused by not being able to see one's loved ones in person; it is possible that spending too much time online and without sufficient human contact played a role; not being able to see one's health care provider may have also been a factor; or, perhaps, a combination of several factors may have impacted overall health in a negative manner.

The data are concerning. A CDC report from August 2020 addressed both the consequences of the pandemic and the consequences of mitigation measures that include social distancing and stay-at-home orders. According to the report, anxiety and depression increased considerably compared to a year before (see Czeisler et al. 2020). We also see from the report that 'elevated levels of adverse mental health conditions, substance use, and suicidal ideation were reported by adults in the United States in June 2020' (Czeisler et al. 2020: par. 7). Another report shows that levels of anxiety, stress and emotional problems have increased among employees as they get ready to return to work (Rodack 2021). In November 2020, risk of general anxiety in women ages 40-59 increased up to 103 per cent (National Alliance of Healthcare 2021). A CDC press release from December 2020 addressing overdose deaths suggests 'an acceleration of overdose deaths during the pandemic' (CDC 2020: par. 2). Increase in mental health issues among the young has been noted (Newsmax 2021). Homicide rates in the US are up more than 30 per cent throughout the country and may be even higher because the data did not include homicide rates in New York and several other large cities (see Reese 2021).

The worrying facts listed in the above paragraph are attributed to the pandemic and to the measures aimed at mitigating it, and it is not possible to tell to what extent increased presence in the digital world contributed to mental and emotional health issues, substance abuse and other unfortunate developments. Some other factors may have also played a role, especially in the rise of homicide rates. In the following section we will take a look at some other developments that will help us understand better the impact of the digital world on human health and relationships.

Digital world and human wellbeing

Studies that provide evidence of links between mental health issues with the presence in the digital world have been around since 2002. Research continues to support the link between mental health issues and increased use of social media (see Nest 2020; Warrender and Milne 2020). Adolescents are especially vulnerable to the influence of social media and electronic device use because they live 'in a media-saturated world, where media is used not only for entertainment purposes, such as listening to music or watching movies, but is also used increasingly for communicating with peers via WhatsApp, Instagram, SnapChat, Facebook, etc.' (Crone and Komijn 2018: par. 1). Nest (2020) lists a variety of risks lurking in the digital world: cyber-bullying and resulting self-harm and suicidal behaviour, social exclusion, social comparison, online conflict and content that promotes risky behaviour. A comprehensive report by Blue Cross Blue Shield notes a surge of depression diagnoses in the US from 2013 through 2016, and especially among adolescent and younger individuals. Video games and use of electronics which also means less time spent in face-to-face interaction appear to play a role (see Hoffman 2018).

Research of adolescents between 2010 and 2015 shows a correlation between screen time and mental health issues. Suicide rates among adolescents have also gone up during the 2010-2015 period. The data also show that digital natives spend more time on media screen activities than on other activities (Twenge, Joiner, Rogers et al. 2018). A national random sample of 2 to 17-year-old children and adolescents in the US in 2016 links increased screen time with lower psychological well-being, higher distractability, lower emotional stability, lower self-control and lower ability to finish tasks. What is of special relevance for the purpose of this paper is that increased screen time is associated with lower ability to make friends (Twenge and Campbell 2018). Two-year-old toddlers already spend over two hours per day of screen time, and some toddlers are already addicted to their tablets. A digital detox centre in the state of Washington named reSTART charges over $500 per day to help young people addicted to electronic devices detox and return to normal life.

In the digital world, we are connected and the opportunities for communication, connections and relationships are many and almost endless. One would, therefore, expect that connections and relationships in the digital world would make us happier and more fulfilled and contribute to our well-being. Interestingly, as illustrated in the previous paragraph, something very different is true. Almost 70 years ago, Ellul wrote:

> In a perpetual monologue by means of which [the human being] escapes the anguish of silence and the inconvenience of neighbors, man [sic] finds refuge in the lap of technique, which envelops him in solitude and at the same time reassures him with all its hoaxes (Ellul 1964: 379-380).

Ellul presciently described what the digital world is doing to us: it provides a sense of refuge and a sense of closeness while at the same time it places us in a perpetual monologue and distances us from other people. In the digital world, we are connected with other people, but without the subtle ties that link us to others, and we are basically alone. Turkle (2012, 2015) writes that technology makes it possible for us to be connected, but that we are actually alone. T. S. Eliot writes in 'The hollow men' about people whose voices are dried and who are 'quiet and meaningless' (Eliot 1925). We need to ask: is that us? Are our voices becoming dried and are we becoming quiet and meaningless as the digital world continues to impact our communication and relationships?

The digital world, similar to technique, has its own life and its own rules and laws. Just like technique, it is practical, effective and efficient. It also contains an objectifying component and it continues on its self-augmenting and self-expanding path. One of the most concerning developments is that the digital world is taking the centre stage and slowly replacing face-to-face communication and interaction. Traditional mediated communication in the form of letters, books, telephone and telegraph has been around for a relatively long time, but it did not replace nor diminish face-to-face communication. Face-to-face communication and traditional mediated communication were two forms of communication that had different functions and complemented one another. Communication in the digital world is very different, Like technique, it expands, absorbs and changes everything. We are to expect that in-person conversations and dialogue will continue to lose relevance and that traditional connections and relationships that presuppose genuine meeting will continue to decline.

Exploring future steps

Research from a number of fields – communication, ethics, psychology and psychiatry – shows that face-to-face contact, interaction and socialising are necessary for developing a healthy personality and building healthy relationships. In ethics, face-to-face meetings and interaction are central. Buber (1965) writes about genuine meeting that he referred to as the *interhuman* or the *between*. It is a meeting that does not rest with one of the persons not with a group. The interhuman is about one person regarding another as a 'partner in a living event' (ibid: 74). According to Buber, 'only in partnership can my being be perceived as an existing whole' (ibid: 75). For Levinas, relationships and responsibility toward the other occur primarily in a face-to-face encounter that enables a partnership and a dialogic relationship. This relationship is at the core of what it means to be human (Levinas 1979; see also Garza and Landrum 2010; Peperzak 1993). Ellul (1964) calls for rehabilitation of the word that presupposes a dialogic and face-to-face encounter.

Buber, Levinas and Ellul lived at a time that precedes our modern-day digital age. One might ask and wonder if they would have considered communication in the digital world to be equal to face-to-face encounters and relationships. Based on their respective writings, a conclusion can be made that genuine human meeting requires face-to-face interaction and that technologically mediated communication would be considered a form of communication that has its place and role in the overall communication process, but not a replacement of in-person encounters. Buber's (1955) distinction among three types of communication can help us understand the relevance of face-to-face communication.

Buber (ibid) distinguishes between monologue disguised as dialogue, technical dialogue and genuine dialogue. He believed that genuine dialogue is what makes us human, and while technical dialogue and monologue have their place in human communication and relationships, they cannot and should not replace genuine dialogue. The digital world provides an abundance of opportunities for monologue and technical dialogue. We also need to be open to the possibility that genuine dialogue may take place in the digital world. We are seeing, for example, an increased number of counselling and medical assistance events in the digital sphere that likely contain elements of genuine dialogue. For the most part, however, the digital world is taking away from us what is inherently human – our ability to understand, empathise and meet others as human beings and maintain sacredness of the other. In the digital world, we want to be heard and we want to exchange information. We also want to form relationships that we can control and that will be pleasant and enjoyable and without the complexity and at times unpleasantness that characterises typical human relationships. None of these are characteristics of genuine dialogue. Furthermore, the digital world creates an interpersonal distance that amplifies objectification and undermines our ethical responsibility toward others. Bogaczyk (2018) links the creation of interpersonal distance with the difference between the visual and oral medium: when we text, send emails, or communicate electronically, we are using visual media. He writes that 'there resides a distance in this type of communication that disconnects us from our relationships with others and releases us from a basic human obligation to the other' (ibid: 93-94). Interpersonal distance in the digital world suggests that conversations, genuine dialogue and human relationships may not be able to thrive in the digital world.

The digital world, like technique, will continue to grow and impact various aspects of our lives. As noted earlier in this essay, when technique enters into human life, it is integrated with humans and becomes the very substance of humans (see Ellul, 1964). Are we, then, to accept the inevitability of the overpowering impact of the technique-centred digital world and passively accept to be absorbed and modified? Are other options available? Can we utilise the practicality, efficiency, effectiveness and convenience of the digital world without allowing it to undermine our humanity?

Overcoming the constraints of the digital world

Ellul's explanations and descriptions of technique are sometimes criticised as having a pessimistic and even a fatalistic tone. While Ellul's explanations, descriptions, illustrations and metaphors may sound pessimistic and fatalistic at times, they provide a detailed understanding and awareness of the workings of technique and its ever-increasing power when untempered by ethical and spiritual considerations. Furthermore, Ellul helps us understand the perils of excessive constraints and passivity imposed by an unbridled technique orientation. His vivid descriptions also encourage reflection and provide hope. For Ellul, hope is rooted in individual responsibility and the need for humans to face their own spiritual imperfections (see Ellul 1973).

In the spirit of hope, we can take specific steps in overcoming the constraints of the digital world. As a starting point, we can apply Ellul's concept of rehabilitation of the word to promote the value of dialogue and face-to-face interaction. Buber's concept of genuine dialogue and Turkle's research on empathy and the need for humans to interact in person with other humans could serve as a basis for explaining the importance of genuine dialogue and face-to-face conversations An explanation of the digital world as a convenient and practical *means* of communication rather than as the central communication medium can also be helpful. We also need to take into account changes that have taken place over the past several years.

The power of the digital world has become formidable and its impact on communication and relationships significant. In-person conversations are becoming a form of interaction with no special relevance and no symbolic meaning. Face-to-face communication and relationships have been changed to such an extent that promoting the values of conversation and genuine dialogue may be understood as suggesting something that is a thing of the past. Calls for embracing digital reality are intensifying (see, e.g., Couros 2015) and augmented reality is being portrayed as the future of humanity. Even counselling is becoming increasingly digital. Ironically, mental and emotional issues that are often caused or exacerbated by spending too much time in the digital world and by not having true human contact are nowadays being treated in the digital world (see Collins 2021). The power and influence of the digital world are rather daunting. And yet, we must continue on the path of hope and personal responsibility.

We need to take a look at our own practices in order to see to what extent we have been influenced by the digital culture and to what extent we still value conversations and genuine dialogue and to what extent we believe that in-person communication, non-mediated empathy and non-mediated compassion are relevant for being human. We can also pay attention to how we interact and communicate with others – whether our in-person communication has been impacted by the digital world to a point that it has turned into a monologue or whether we find the time to engage in conversations and dialogue. We can also remind ourselves of Ellul's concept of technique and attempt to determine to what extent we have allowed the constraining aspects of technique to govern our communication and relationships. We also need to keep in mind that technique has its positives – it is practical, efficient and convenient, and we need to make an effort to use it to our own benefit without allowing it to diminish and desacralise our humanity.

Conclusion

Using technology to better human life is a wonderful development. Numerous advancements in technology have made our lives more enjoyable, healthier and safer. They have also resulted in the emergence of the digital world which is practical, convenient and pleasurable. The problem is that we, humans, have allowed ourselves to become dependent on technology and that technology is shaping the manner in which we communicate with others, live and form relationships with others. We are not only immersed in the digital world to a smaller or larger extent – we are allowing the digital world to shape and mold our communication, our relationships and who we are as humans.

Ellul's technique is a complex and somewhat elusive concept that draws attention to the limitations, constraints and spiritual paucity brought about by a value system that disregards the spiritual and enhances efficiency, effectiveness, speed, progress, rationality and practicality. While these values are positive and have helped improve the conditions and standards of living, their excessive application in every aspect of human life leads to a world in which everything – nature, animals, humans, the environment – become means to an end.

In this paper, Ellul's technique was used as a starting point for discussing communication and relationships at a time of increased use of communication technology and the emergence of a digital reality and its technique-based value system. An attempt was made to answer the question whether conversations and genuine dialogue which are the basis of human relationships are possible in a world influenced by the values of technique.

The digital world is not a copy of what can traditionally be considered the real world. It is a world of its own and a world with its own rules and laws. The digital world will continue to expand as access to the internet and communication devices become more and more available to the whole planet, and it will continue to impact what can traditionally be considered the real world – the non-digital world.

Most of us belong to the digital world to some extent because it is practical, convenient, effective and efficient and because it helps us stay connected. We should not forget, however, that being human is much more than practicality, convenience, effectiveness and efficiency, and that a more profound connection exists that requires in-person meetings, conversations and dialogue. Ellul's 'fish of the deep' is a metaphor that we can use to understand the relevance of the sacred, beautiful and mysterious in human communication and human relationships

References

Arendt, H. (1958) *The human condition*, Chicago, University of Chicago Press

Arnett, R. C. (1986) *Communication and community: Implications of Martin Buber's dialogue*, Carbondale, Southern Illinois University Press

Arnett, R. C. and Arneson, P. (1999) *Dialogic civility in a cynical age: Community, hope, and interpersonal relationships*, New York, State University of New York Press

Bogaczyk, J. S. (2018) The word: Jacques Ellul's dialogic response to la technique. Unpublished dissertation, Duquesne University Duquesne Scholarship Collection. Available online at https://dsc.duq.edu/cgi/viewcontent.cgi?article=2458&context=etd

Buber, M. (1955) *Between man and man,* Boston, Beacon Press

Buber, M. (1958) *I and thou*, trans by Smith, R. G., New York, Scribner, second edition

Buber, M. (1965) *The knowledge of man*, London, G. Allen & Unwin

CDC (2020) Overdose deaths accelerating during Covid-19, press release, 17 December. Available online at https://www.cdc.gov/media/releases/2020/p1218-overdose-deaths-covid-19.html

Collins, T. (2021) Survey finds young Americans are using social media to address mental health issues ... caused by social media, Medical Press, 17 March. Available online at https://medicalxpress.com/news/2021-03-survey-young-americans-social-media.html

Common Sense Media (2015) The Common Sense census: Media use by tweens and teens, 3 November. Available online at https://www.commonsensemedia.org/the-common-sense-census-media-use-by-tweens-and-teens-infographic

Common Sense Media (2019) The Common Sense Census: Media use by tweens and teens. Available online at https://www.commonsensemedia.org/research/the-common-sense-census-media-use-by-tweens-and-teens-2019

Couros, A. (2015) Identity in a digital world, TedTalks, 17 January. Available online at https://www.youtube.com/watch?v=pAllBTgYfDo

Crone. E. A. and Konijn, E. A. (2018) Media use and brain development during adolescence, *Nature Communications*, 21 February. Available online at https://www.ncbi.nlm.nih.gov/pmc/articles/PMC5821838/ DOI 10.1038/s41467-018-03126-x

Czeisler, M. E., Lane, L. I., Petrosky, E., Wiley, J. F., Christensen, A., Njai, R. et al. (2020) Mental health, substance use, and suicidal ideation during the Covid-19 Pandemic – United States, 24-30 June 2020, CDC, 14 August. Available online at https://www.cdc.gov/mmwr/volumes/69/wr/mm6932a1.htm

Digital Humans (2021) Deloitte. Available online at https://www2.deloitte.com/nl/nl/pages/customer-and-marketing/articles/digital-human.html

Eisenberg, E. M., Trethewey, A., LeGreco, M. and Goodall, L. H., Jr. (2017) *Organizational communication: Balancing creativity and constraint*, Boston, Bedford/St. Martin's, eighth edition

Eliot, T. S. (1925) The hollow men. Available online at https://allpoetry.com/the-hollow-men

Ellul, J. (1964) *The technological society*, trans. by Wilkinson, J., New York, Vintage Books. Available online at https://ratical.org/ratville/AoS/TheTechnologicalSociety.pdf

Ellul, J. (1973) *Hope in time of abandonment*, trans by Hopkin, C. E., New York, Seabury Press

Ellul, J. (1980) *The technological system*, trans by Neugroschel, J., New York, The Continuum Publishing Corp. Available online at http://www.newhumanityinstitute

Ellul, J. (1985) *The humiliation of the word*, trans by Hanks, J. M., Grand Rapids, MI, Eerdmans

Ellul, J. (2019) Video: Jacques Ellul – Interview 1979 w/subtitles, 13 May. Available online at https://www.youtube.com/watch?v=lwL0BJek2bc

Eyesafe (2020) Covid-19 screen time spikes to over 13 hours per day according to Eyesafe Nielsen estimates. Available online at https://eyesafe.com/covid-19-screen-time-spike-to-over-13-hours-per-day/

Foreman, C. (2017) 10 types of social media and how each can benefit your business, hootsuite.com

Fromm, E. (1956) *The art of loving*, New York, Harper and Row

Garza, G. and Landrum, B. (2010) Ethics and the primacy of the Other: A Levinasian foundation for phenomenological research, *Indo-Pacific Journal of Phenomenology*, Vol. 2, No. 2 pp 1-12

Geertz, C. (1973) *The interpretation of cultures*, New York, Basic Books

Gillies, T. (2017) Why most of Three Square Market's employees jumped at the chance to wear a microchip, *CNBC*, 13 August. Available online at https://www.cnbc.com/2017/08/11/three-square-market-ceo-explains-its-employee-microchip-implant.html

Hoffman, B. (2018) Report: Depression is sky rocketing in America, *Newsmax*, 10 May. Available online at https://www.newsmax.com/newsfront/survey-depression-surge america/2018/05/10/id/859531/

Levinas, E. (1979) Totality and infinity: An essay on exteriority, trans by Lingis, A., The Hague, Martinus Nijhoff Publishers

Matlock, S. (2014) Confronting the technological society: On Jacques Ellul's classic analysis of technique, *The New Atlantis*. Available online at https://www.thenewatlantis.com/publications/confronting-the-technological-society

Montagu, A. and Matson, F. (1983) *The dehumanization of man*, New York, McGraw-Hill

National Alliance of Healthcare (2021) Women's risk of addiction up 65% according to Mental Health Index, National Alliance of Healthcare Purchases Coalition. Available online at https://www.nationalalliancehealth.org/www/news/news-press-releases/mental-health-index-december-2020

Nesi, J. (2020) The impact of social media on youth mental health: Challenges and opportunities, *North Carolina Medical Journal*, Vol. 81, No. 2 pp 116-121. DOI 10.18043/ncm.81.2.116

Newsmax (2021) Pandemic has depression, anxiety rates among youth climbing worldwide, 10 August. Available online at https://www.newsmax.com/health/health-news/pandemic-mental-health-depression-anxiety/2021/08/10/id/1031740/

Peperzak, A. (1993) To the Other: An introduction to the philosophy of Emmanuel Levinas, West Lafayette, IN, Purdue University Press E-Books. Available online at http://docs.lib.purdue.edu/purduepress_ebooks/20/

Reese, P. (2021) Homicides surge 27% in California in 2020 amid COVID shutdowns of schools, youth programs, *DesertSun*, 16 May. Available online at https://www.desertsun.com/story/news/nation/california/2021/05/16/homicides-surged-27-california-2020-during-covid-19-pandemic/5096101001/

Rodack, J. (2021) Employees' mental health worsens as they prepare to return to workplaces, *Newsmax*, 21 May. Available online at https://www.newsmax.com/us/employees-mental-health-index-workplace/2021/05/21/id/1022235/

Samuely, A. (n.d.) Speedo's new swimming app serves as a training partner, *MarketingDive*. Available online at https://www.marketingdive.com/ex/mobilemarketer/cms/news/manufacturers/18741.html

Statista (n.d.) Number of email users worldwide. Available online at https://www.statista.com/statistics/255080/number-of-e-mail-users-worldwide

Turkle, S. (2012) *Alone together: Why we expect more from technology and less from each other*, New York, Basic Books

Turkle, S. (2015) *Reclaiming conversation: The power of talk in a digital age*, New York, Penguin Press

Twenge, J. M., Joiner, T. L. Rogers, M. L. et al. (2018) Increases in depressive symptoms, suicide-related outcomes, and suicide rates among US adolescents after 2010 and links to increased new media screen time, *Clinical Psychological Science*, Vol. 6, No.1 pp 3-17. DOI 10.1177/2167702617723376

Twenge, J. M. and Campbell, K. W. (2018) Associations between screen time and lower psychological well-being among children and adolescents: Evidence from a population-based study, *Prev Med Rep*, Vol. 12 pp 271-283, DOI 10.1016/j.pmedr.2018.10.003

Vogels, A. and Anderson, M. (2020) Dating and Relationships in the Digital Age, Pew Research Center, 8 May. Available online at https://www.pewresearch.org/internet/2020/05/08/dating-and-relationships-in-the-digital-age/

Warrender, D. and Milne, R. (2020) How use of social media and social comparison affect mental health, *Nursing Times*, Vol. 116, No. 3 pp 56-59. Available online at https://www.nursingtimes.net/news/mental-health/how-use-of-social-media-and-social-comparison-affect-mental-health-24-02-2020/

Werner, J. (2017) Augmented reality, TEDxAsburyPark, 3 August. Available online at https://www.youtube.com/watch?v=RDvBowq3ed8

Whatsnew2Day (2021) Speedo's Intelligent swimsuit could help swimmers go 4% faster by 2040, WhatsNew2Day, 15 June. Available online at https://whatsnew2day.com/speedos-intelligent-swimsuit-could-help-swimmers-go-4-faster-by-2040/

Note on the contributor

Slavica Kodish, PhD., is a Professor of Communication Studies at Southeast Missouri State University. She teaches organisational communication, leadership communication and related courses. Her research interests include organisational trust, ethics, dialogue and application of communication theory. Her publications appear in the *International Journal of Business Communication*; *Journal of Organizational Psychology*; *International Journal of Communication*; *Journal of Education for Business*; *American Communication Journal*; *Journal of Relationship Marketing*, and more. She received various awards, including the outstanding advisor award, female faculty of the year award and top paper awards.

Susanne Fengler
Monika Lengauer
Anna Carina Zappe

Introducing the new UNESCO handbook, *Reporting on migrants and refugees*

Introduction

Unprecedented numbers of people are on the move in modern times. As of mid-2020, the United Nations counted more than 280 million international migrants – 3.6 per cent of the world's population (UNDESA 2020: 1). Journalists and journalism educators have a responsibility to understand this phenomenon and to report accurately, ethically and appropriately, both in receiving and sending countries. Yet, as we detail below, balanced reporting is rare and the issue easily exploited. This handbook provides an interdisciplinary curriculum on the multiple aspects of migration with the aim of enabling users to report proficiently and responsibly about a complex field that impacts all lives – an issue even more important as the war in Ukraine creates a new wave of refugees.

The scale of migration

These numbers were collected before the Russian aggression on Ukraine which started on 24 February 2022. The military offensive triggered the 'fastest growing refugee crisis in Europe since World War II' (Grandi 2019). More than 10 million people were forcibly displaced either internally – those who sought shelter elsewhere in the country as internally displaced persons (IDPs) in Ukraine – or across borders as refugees (IDMC 2022; UNHCR 2022a). When crossing borders in search of protection, their first move took most refugees to Poland, but also to Romania, the Republic of Moldova and Hungary (UNHCR 2022b) before many continued onwards to other countries, mainly in Europe.

Already the 'refugee crisis' of 2015-2016 had made a deep impact on public debate and political landscapes across and beyond Europe.

During this period almost 2.5 million asylum-seekers submitted asylum claims in the European Union (EU). Images of refugees from the Syrian civil war making their way towards Europe on foot became iconic, as did those of ships in the Mediterranean Sea overloaded with African migrants and refugees. Around one million asylum applicants from sub-Saharan African countries were registered in Europe between 2010 and 2017, with 'dramatically' rising numbers (Connor 2018).

Large movements of refugees and migrants have political, economic, social, developmental, humanitarian and human rights ramifications. Migration is a cross-cultural and interdisciplinary subject that requires journalists to have knowledge of an array of complex and interrelated matters. The UN Global Compact for Migration, passed in 2018, states that media professionals should be 'sensitised' and 'educated' for migration-related issues and terminology, in order to provide 'independent, objective and quality reporting' guided by 'ethical reporting standards … in full respect for the freedom of the media'.

Migration and forced displacement: Debates in origin and destination countries

Before the war in Ukraine, the discussion on migration and asylum policies had a considerable impact on election outcomes across Europe, shedding light on a sharp divide between EU countries (Harteveld et al. 2018), including the impact of different migration histories. While the former colonial powers France and the United Kingdom (UK) have had decades-long experiences as destination countries for migrants and refugees, after the end of World War Two in 1945 other European countries (e.g. Italy, Spain, Portugal and Greece) experienced both outward migration of their nationals (mainly to north-western European countries) and inward migration, in addition to providing protection to refugees. After the fall of the Iron Curtain in 1990, countries in central and eastern Europe (e.g. Poland, the Czech Republic) also experienced both outward migration of their nationals (mainly to other European countries) and inward migration. In Poland, inward migration originated mainly from Ukraine (Boswell and Geddes 2011; UNDESA 2019a) just as Poland was the first safe haven for many Ukrainian refugees following the Russian offensive of 2022.

Top migration issues besides Ukraine, at the time of writing, remain the Syrian, Iraqi and the Venezuelan situations, according to the Migration Policy Institute, as well as the sheer numbers overall (IOM 2019; UNDESA 2019b; UNHCR 2020). In Africa, migration is significantly increasing in all directions: numbers are growing for migration between countries on the continent and particularly for migration from the continent, in this case especially to Europe (IOM, McAuliffe and Triandafyllidou 2022: 56, 60-61). Connor (2018) reveals this, in international terms, to be an unusual African trend. By comparing data from 1990 and 2017, he shows that the proportion of intra-African migrants has decreased by 7 percentage points between 1990 and 2017 (from 75 per cent to 68

Susanne Fengler

Monika
Lengauer

Anna Carina
Zappe

per cent), and the proportion of Africans who exited the continent has increased – migration to Europe has grown by 6 percentage points from 11 per cent to 17 per cent, and to the US by 4 percentage points from 2 per cent to 6 per cent. The IOM also emphasises this development (IOM et al. 2022: 56, 60-61).

The issue also remains high on the media agendas of the United States, the United Kingdom and the Russian Federation, as other key destination countries for migrants in the global north. The US remains home to the highest absolute number of international migrants (IOM et al. 2022: 24-25), and the media pay tribute to the topic, with a special focus on the situation at the US border with Mexico (Kreutler, Maier, Diop, Miller and Ravisankar 2021). Before the invasion of Ukraine in February 2022, Russia had been among the top five countries attracting migrants, and it has at the same time been among the top five sending countries (IOM et al. 2022: 24-25). Immigrants mainly came from former Soviet republics (UNDESA 2019), while emigrants often comprised of well-educated specialists whose decision to leave was ascribed to the increase of authoritarian trends and perceived suppression of freedom of speech and entrepreneurship since 2000. However, the motifs of these Russian emigrants, who left the country because of growing political pressure, have not been thematised in the Russian public discussion (Herbst and Erofeev 2019).

Saudi Arabia, a 'high-income economy' according to the World Bank classification (World Bank n.d.), is among the top five destination countries for migrants, but not for refugees (IOM et al. 2022: 24-25). The profile of the Arab world regarding migration and forced displacement is very diverse. On the one hand, the high-income economies of the Arab Gulf countries attract labour migrants from all parts of the world (ibid: 75). A lack of economic opportunities pushes nationals from many north African and Middle Eastern countries away in order to make a living elsewhere. War and conflict in Iraq, Libya, Palestine, Syria, Yemen generate some of the major refugee populations of our times.

Some countries, such as Morocco and Tunisia, have a dual profile of sending and receiving migrants. The lack of freedoms in the Arab World often restricts an unbiased and responsible reporting of the issues (Hamdy and Ali 2021). In Asia, migration is multifaceted. Labour migration results in high amounts of international remittances, with India and China as main recipients while the Philippines, Pakistan and Bangladesh are also largely reliant on these funds. Disasters – earthquakes, floods, storms and other climate-related and geophysical events – as well as conflicts, for instance in Afghanistan and Myanmar, are responsible for massive forced displacements internally and across borders. Countries such as Afghanistan, Bangladesh, Indonesia, Myanmar, Pakistan and the Philippines are among the top 20 migrant and refugee sending countries globally (IOM et al. 2022: 25, Figure 2 pp 39-44, 73-87). Reporting on these issues is largely restricted by curbs on freedom of expression (Khan 2021; Kurkowski 2021).

Context factors for migration need to be covered more comprehensively

Emigration is frequently ascribed to a lack of alternatives (Giménez-Gómez, Walle and Zewdu 2019) and also sharp rises of the population (Kebede, Goujon and Lutz 2019). Remittances sent home by migrants continue to represent a substantial share of the national GDPs in many countries (World Bank 2018). In a 'global society', transnational migration and mobility are also considered beneficial for crowded labour markets in countries of origin and destination countries in need of labour (Sassen 2007).

The scale of migration demands sound reflection in journalism education. Journalists have a responsibility to acquire knowledge in the field of migration and mobility, to comprehend its complexity, to use accurate data from reliable sources and to apply appropriate reporting techniques. They need to report ethically and they also need to be aware of the fact that local news is interwoven with regional and international developments. Journalism educators have a responsibility to train journalism students for these tasks. We also argue that it is extremely relevant to focus on news media coverage of migration in countries of origin of migration. Communication (including journalistic media, social media, personal communication between migrants and their co-ethnic communities, migratory peers, diaspora etc.) is a factor of outstanding relevance in explaining migration and mobility. However, across continents, we currently observe a lack of quality coverage. A lack of (balanced) public debate can easily be exploited by political actors with strategic interests.

This is where our handbook for journalism educators, *Reporting on migrants and refugees*, comes in. It was first published by UNESCO in English in 2021, to be followed by Arabic, French, Kiswahili and Spanish editions. Researched and edited by the Erich Brost Institute for International Journalism at the TU Dortmund University, Germany, the handbook is concerned in the first instance with media coverage of people – migrants, refugees, internally displaced persons (IDPs), stateless people and their host communities. In addition, it is set in the context of migration and development. The interdisciplinary curriculum comprises all aspects needed to train journalistic analysis, research, presentation, editorial marketing and ethics of migration coverage. It addresses journalism educators in the global south as well as in the global north, media federations and associations and it reaches out to those who report on migrants and refugees in newsrooms. It is available, open access, from the UNESCO homepage (Fengler, Lengauer and Zappe 2021).

Key issues in African countries

Factors triggering migration decisions range from poor governance and corruption, conflict and climate change to the perceived lack of individual chances. In addition, a lack of economic opportunities,

Susanne Fengler

Monika
Lengauer

Anna Carina
Zappe

inequities and gender-related issues are considered key factors for migration. Growing migrant numbers are proof of the urgent need in many societies and governments especially in the global south to act to improve the opportunities of citizens at home. Eric Chinje, one of the continent's best-known journalists and former head of the African Media Initiative, argues that, as long as migration is not adequately covered in African countries, one may never see a critical constituency that fights for policies to effectively address root causes of (illegal) migration. Rising social, economic and environmental inequalities have been exacerbated by the Covid-19 pandemic. Indeed, the pandemic's impact is harshest for people on the move, such as migrants in irregular situations, migrant workers with precarious livelihoods and people fleeing because of persecution, war, violence, human rights violations or disaster, whether within their own countries as IDPs or across international borders as refugees and asylum-seekers. Journalists face even more challenging conditions due to Covid-19 including 'lower incomes, especially for freelances and limited access to venues', according to the European Commission's first-ever 'Recommendation to strengthen the safety of journalists and other media professionals' (European Commission 2021).

In a series of workshops with leading African journalism educators involved in this project (financed by the Robert Bosch Foundation between 2017 and 2020), the handbook's project team has jointly identified the following specific challenges to journalism education and newsrooms in African countries addressed in the handbook:

- a lack of skills and resources for investigative research on migration matters;

- a lack of knowledge on key topics relevant for the development of African societies;

- a lack of 'African stories' and dominance of international news wire material;

- a lack of intra-African journalists' networks to cover cross-border matters of migration, and

- a lack of entrepreneurial skills needed to find a market for critical and complex stories.

In exploratory workshops conducted by the consortium (financed by the German foreign office between 2015 and 2020), African journalists involved in these workshops have confirmed the above shortcomings in their reporting realities. Of the over 100 participants in workshops in Ghana, Guinea, Ivory Coast and Nigeria, many had no prior experience with migration as a topic of reporting and had not linked the phenomena to questions of development. Participants also alluded to a lack of awareness about the difficulties that migrants faced in European destination countries. They also assessed that even though African citizens might be aware of the dangers of irregular migration, the expected positive outcomes of migration to Europe – remittances and financial benefits for the family as well as gains in reputation – outweighed these risks. This is corroborated by empirical studies, such as the UNDP study *Scaling fences* (UNDP 2019). Similarly, the actual African migrants we have interviewed for our research state that migration is mostly 'a forgotten story' in the local media (Bastian et al. 2018).

Coverage of migration in origin versus destination countries

The handbook is built on two multi-country comparative analyses of news coverage in refugees' and migrants' destination countries and countries of origin. Our data from a comparative study of migration coverage in 22 African and European news outlets shows that the actual migrants receive more attention in destination countries than in origin countries. In contrast to coverage in European media, coverage by African media centred on politicians (20.8 per cent) and representatives of international organisations (23.8 per cent). Citizens, including actual or potential migrants, played a minor role (12.5 per cent), as did civil society representatives (14.9 per cent). Telling the 'African migration story' would also imply that coverage in Africa starts to include the actual migrants – but in our sample, less than one in ten articles published by the African news outlets featured a migrant or refugee as main actor.

According to the study of 1,512 articles, the topic was much less salient in African countries, with only 175 articles found in the African news outlets under study. This confirms previous studies pointing towards a higher salience of the topic of migration in the destination countries of migrants (e.g. Assopgoum 2011; Eberl at al. 2019). Coverage in European destination countries was dominated by domestic issues like border security and migration policy, but also paid attention to the actual migrants – who received much less coverage in the origin countries. Spectacular boat accidents and disasters – involving many African victims – in the Mediterranean receive by far the highest attention in African media (9.7 per cent). Both African and European media ignored the causes of migration.

Thus, the study shows that migration is severely under-reported in African countries, while it suffers from one-dimensional and self-centred perspectives in Europe. To a considerable extent, the news agenda of African media mirrors the European news agenda, clearly demonstrating that African media so far fail to tell the 'African story' of migration. This is also true for the choice of countries of coverage as well as actors, which are disproportionally often from Europe rather than from Africa. There is even more attention devoted to European migration policies (4.6 per cent) and frontier security (in Europe) (2.9 per cent) in African media than to the coverage of national migration politics (2.3 per cent) pertinent to each African country. Numerous aspects potentially relevant to an African audience receive little coverage. Causes of migration in

Susanne Fengler

Monika
Lengauer

Anna Carina
Zappe

general, poor governance, poverty, climate change, lack of security and other key push factors are only rarely covered as main topics by African media in the context of migration to Europe (5.8 per cent). Migration routes received more attention from European media (5.3 per cent) than African media (2.9 per cent). Our study results clearly show that journalism education needs to provide training to the future generation of journalists. The aim is for them to overlook no longer the economic and socio-political realities driving people to move away from home.

Coverage of refugees and migrants in Europe

Our second comparative study on coverage of migrants and refugees in 17 countries has been built on a dataset of 2,417 news articles published in six sample weeks between 2015 and 2018 – in fifteen European countries plus the United States and Russia (Fengler and Kreutler 2020; Fengler et al. 2020). The data involved two agenda-setting print or online media outlets per country. The study indicates the need to train also European journalists for a research-based and comprehensive coverage of refugee and migration matters – because until the Ukraine war, which brought matters of forced displacement back into the heart of Europe, media in many European countries covered migrants and refugees only in the context of foreign coverage.

Comparing key topic areas over the six study weeks in our analysis also revealed remarkably different patterns of coverages between western and central-eastern European (CEE) countries before the Ukraine war. The overall shares of articles focusing on politics and context information were similar in western EU and CEE countries. However, media outlets in CEE countries report notably more on problems with migrants and protests against them. Analysed over time, the share of articles on situation and help (situation, personal stories, support) was highest both in western (36.1 per cent) and eastern (37.5 per cent) EU media in the first study week of August/September 2015. The share of articles on problems and protests in western EU coverage is continuously lower than in CEE countries, and in five out of six weeks also than in Russian and USA media.

Looking at coverage of problems and protests in all six study weeks, the topic occupied substantially more room in media with a conservative profile across Europe, as well as in outlets in eastern Europe in general. The coverage of the situation and help provided the refugees had a very high share in liberal media in western Europe. Coverage in liberal/left-wing media in CEE countries was less consistent in this regard and increasingly focused on problems and protests from 2016. The strongest focus on the situation and help provided can be found in western EU liberal media, which published 4.9 times more articles on these rather neutral or even positive aspects, compared to the coverage of – rather negatively framed – situation and help than on problems and protests. This rate was 1.5 in western EU conservative/right-wing media, 2.0 in eastern EU liberal and 1.4 in eastern EU conservative media.

The study also included the analysis of perspectives (domestic/foreign news/foreign news with national involvement) and directions of the migration and refugee movements reported in an article. Generally, eastern EU media reported less from a domestic coverage perspective (23.1 per cent; western EU: 35.9 per cent) and on migration into other European countries (72.3 per cent), while western EU (35.3 per cent) and particularly US media (46.8 per cent) reported more on migration into their own countries. In contrast, many outlets in both western and central eastern Europe covered migrants and refugees as remote phenomena, as movements into other countries on the continent. Foreign coverage of the topic was, for example, the dominant pattern in Poland and the Czech Republic. While Portugal, Romania, Poland and the Czech Republic are all countries with comparably low absolute numbers of first-time asylum applications, Spanish media also covered the topic predominantly as foreign coverage: these results are especially relevant as our analysis shows that the perspective of the articles is linked to topic selection. Articles dealing with support for migrants and refugees are more frequent in domestic (12.1 per cent) than in foreign coverage (5 per cent). Problems with migrants are reported more frequently in foreign (12.9 per cent) than in domestic coverage (6.5 per cent).

Perspectives

The message is clear: many newsrooms in Europe may also be challenged to cover adequately the longer-term impact of the Ukrainian war and refugee movement into European countries. Our handbook wants to give them guidance as well. Specific modules train journalists how to generate story ideas, pitch a story to editors in charge of commissioning journalistic assignments, and use social media to address larger audiences for migration-related stories. We have also piloted a MOOC (massive open online course) on media and migration (available in German) commissioned by the German federal chancellery, available since March 2022 (www.medien-migration-integration.de) and hope to be able to translate this new e-learning tool into further European languages in the near future.

References

Assopgoum, F. T. (2011) *Migration aus Afrika in die EU: Eine Analyse der Berichterstattung in deutschen und senegalesischen Zeitungen* [*Migration from Africa to the EU: An analysis of reporting in German and Senegalese newspapers*], Wiesbaden, VS Verlag für Sozialwissenschaften

Bastian, M., Zappe, A.-C., Wüllner, G., Oppermann, L., Leißner, L., Henke, J. and Serwornoo, M. (2018) *Abschlussbericht Auswärtiges Amt: Evaluationsprojekt zur Qualität der aktuellen Berichterstattung in afrikanischen Schlüssel-ländern* [*Final report of the Federal Foreign Office: Evaluation project on the quality of current reporting in key African countries*], EBI Working Paper 2018. Internal Document

Boswell, C. and Geddes, A. (2011) *Migration and mobility in the European Union*, New York, Palgrave Macmillan

Susanne Fengler

Monika Lengauer

Anna Carina Zappe

Connor, P. (2018) At least a million sub-Saharan Africans moved to Europe since 2010: Sub-Saharan migration to the United States also growing, Pew Research Center, 22 March. Available online at http://assets.pewresearch.org/wp-content/uploads/sites/2/2018/03/22135249/Africa-Migration-March-22-FULL-REPORT.pdf

Eberl, J.-M., Galyga, S., Lind, F., Heidenreich, T., Edie, R., Boomgaarden, H. G., Herrero, B, Gómez Montero, E. L. and Berganza, R. (2019) European media migration report: How media cover migration and intra-EU mobility in terms of salience, sentiment and framing. Available online at https://www.reminder-project.eu/wp-content/uploads/2019/08/REMINDER-D8.3.pdf, accessed on 20 December 2020

European Commission (2021) Recommendation to strengthen the safety of journalists and other media professionals, 16 September. Available online at https://digital-strategy.ec.europa.eu/en/library/recommendation-protection-safety-and-empowerment-journalists, accessed on 12 January 2023

Fengler, S., Lengauer, M. and Zappe, A.-C. (eds) (2021) *Reporting on migrants and refugees: Handbook for journalism educators*, Paris, UNESCO

Fengler, S. and Kreutler, M. (2020) Migration coverage in Europe's media: A comparative analysis of coverage in 17 countries, Frankfurt/Main, OBS Working Paper 39. Available online at https://www.otto-brenner-stiftung.de/fileadmin/user_data/stiftung/02_Wissenschaftsportal/03_Publikationen/AP39_Migration_EN.pdf, accessed on 20 December 2020

Fengler, S., Bastian, M., Brinkmann, J., Zappe, A.-C., Tatah, V., Andindilile, M., Assefa, E., Chibita, M., Mbaine, A., Obonyo, L., Quashigah, T., Skleparis, D., Splendore, S., Tadesse, M. and Lengauer, M. (2020) Covering migration – in Africa and Europe: Results from a comparative analysis of 11 countries, *Journalism Practice*, Vol. 16, No. 1 pp 140-160. Available online at https://doi.org/10.1080/17512786.2020.1792333

Giménez-Gómez, J. M., Walle, Y. M. and Zewdu, Y. (2019) Trends in African migration to Europe: Drivers beyond economic motivations, *Journal of Conflict Resolution*, Vol. 63, No. 8 pp 1797-1831. Available online at https://doi.org/10.1177/0022002718823907

Grandi, F. (2019) The global compact on refugees: A historic achievement, *International Migration*, Vol. 57, No. 6 pp 23-26. Available online at https://doi.org/10.1111/imig.12671

Hamdy, N. and Ali, A. G. (2021) Perspectives from Egypt: Intra-African migration to Egypt, Fengler, S. and Lengauer, M. (eds) *Reporting on media, migration and forced displacement: Global perspectives*, Erich Brost Institute for International Journalism, TU Dortmund University pp 10-12

Harteveld, E., Schaper, J., Lange, S. L. de and van der Brug, W. (2018) Blaming Brussels? The impact of (news about) the refugee crisis on attitudes towards the EU and national politics, *JCMS: Journal of Common Market Studies*, Vol. 56, No. 1 pp 157-177. Available online at https://doi.org/10.1111/jcms12664

Herbst, J. E. and Erofeev, S. (2019) The Putin exodus: The new Russian brain drain: A report, Atlantic Council. Available online at https://www.atlanticcouncil.org/in-depth-research-reports/report/the-putin-exodus-the-new-russian- brain-drain-3/, accessed on 18 December 2020

Internal Displacement Monitoring Center (IDMC) (2022) Ukraine. Available online at https://www.internal-displacement.org/countries/ukraine

IOM (2019) *World migration report 2020*, Geneva, IOM. Available online at https://publications.iom.int/system/files/pdf/wmr_2020.pdf, accessed on 15 December 2020

IOM, McAuliffe, M. and Triandafyllidou, A. (2022) *World migration report 2022*, Geneva, IOM. Available online at https://publications.iom.int/books/world-migration-report-2022, accessed on 27 April 2022

Kebede, E., Goujon, A. and Lutz, W. (2019) Stalls in Africa's fertility decline partly result from disruptions in female education, *Proceedings of the National Academy of Sciences of the United States of America*, Vol. 116, No. 8 pp 2891-2896. Available online at https://doi.org/10.1073/pnas.1717288116

Khan, Sher Baz (2021) Perspectives from Pakistan, Fengler, S. and Lengauer, M. (eds) *Reporting on media, migration and forced displacement: Global perspectives*, Erich Brost Institute for International Journalism, TU Dortmund University pp 22-23

Kreutler, M., Maier, S., Diop, L., Bane, K. and Ravisankar, R. (2021) How media in the US cover migrants and refugees, Fengler, S. and Lengauer, M. (eds) *Reporting on media, migration and forced displacement: Global perspectives*, Erich Brost Institute for International Journalism, TU Dortmund University pp 29-31

Kurkowski, I. (2021) Perspectives from Asia, Fengler, S. and Lengauer, M. (eds) *Reporting on media, migration and forced displacement: Global perspectives*, Erich Brost Institute for International Journalism, TU Dortmund University pp 18-21

Sassen, S. (2007) *A sociology of globalization: Contemporary societies*, New York, Norton

UNDESA (2019a) Country profile: Germany: International migrant stock. Available online at https://www.un.org/en/development/desa/population/migration/data/estimates2/countryprofiles.asp, accessed on 5 December 2020

UNDESA (2019b) *World population prospects 2019, Volume I: Comprehensive tables*, New York, United Nations Available online at https://population.un.org/wpp/Publications/Files/WPP2019_Volume-I_Comprehensive-Tables.pdf, accessed on 30 July 2020

UNDESA (2020) *International migration 2020: Highlights,* New York, United Nations. Available online at https://www.un.org/development/desa/pd/sites/www.un.org.development.desa.pd/files/undesa_pd_2020_international_migration_highlights.pdf, accessed on 13 December 2020

UNDP (2019) *Scaling fences: Voices of irregular African migrants to Europe*, New York, UNDP. Available online at https://www.africa.undp.org/content/rba/en/home/library/reports/ScalingFences.html, accessed on 13 December 2020

UNHCR (2020) Global trends: Forced displacement in 2019. Available online at https://www.unhcr.org/5ee200e37.pdf, accessed on 15 December 2020

UNHCR (2022a) Ukraine refugee situation. Available online at https://data2.unhcr.org/en/situations/ukraine

UNHCR (2022b) Ukraine situation: Flash update #5. Available online at https://data2.unhcr.org/en/situations/ukraine

World Bank (n.d.) World Bank country and lending groups: Country classification. Available online at World Bank website: https://datahelpdesk.worldbank.org/knowledgebase/articles/906519-world-bank-country-and-lending-groups

World Bank (2018) Migration and remittances: Recent developments and outlook. Special topic: transit migration. Available online at https://www.knomad.org/sites/default/files/2018-04/Migration%20and%20Development%20Brief%2029.pdf, accessed on 16 December 2020

Notes on the contributors

Dr Susanne Fengler is Professor for International Journalism at the Technical University Dortmund and Scientific Director of the Erich Brost Institute for International Journalism at TU Dortmund University, Germany. Monika Lengauer and Anna-Carina Zappe are senior researchers at the Erich Brost Institute for International Journalism (EBI) at TU Dortmund University, Germany.

Emotions and virtues in feature writing: The alchemy of creating prize-winning stories

Jennifer Martin

Palgrave Macmillan, 2021 pp 270

ISBN: 9783030629786 (hbk); 9783030629786 (ebk)

This text interrogates notions close to my heart. For years I have been reading and analysing how some long-form writing is just so good that we never forget it and can summon-up visuals of the narrative as if we were there, sometimes years later. Beautiful, elegant, mostly simple writing that sings off the page.

Martin delves into this abstract and mysterious space, asking simply how journalists evoke an emotional response in their readers? Using three case studies of Walkley award-winning writers (two of them not necessarily identifying as journalists), she analyses their writing, charting it against her own Virtue Map for technical elements and crossovers.

Pivoting off the notion of virtue ethics, Martin's Virtue Map is an inspired attempt to get to the heart of the matter; an 'analytical framework tool' (p. 99) consisting of six fundamentals or, as she writes, 'coordinates': courage, empathy, honesty, responsibility, resilience and phronesis (defined by Aristotle as practical wisdom) (p. xiii).

The text is divided into two sections: Section 1 simply entitled 'Theory' and Section 2, 'Case studies'. Chapter 1 sets out an overview and rationale of her work. Chapter 2 takes us back beyond Tom Wolfe, Dickens and Defoe to Greek myths emanating from Athens of the fifth century BC, with a theoretical element explaining the premise behind journalism prizes and awards, and their place in society. Chapter 3 introduces us to her newly-theorised Virtue Paradigm, used by Martin to rationalise her virtue mapping. It is a theoretical yet eclectic deep dive into further grand notions swirling around the rendering of narrative journalism and its role within society. Chapter 4 is an explanation of all research methods applied including textual, discourse and critical analyses. And interestingly, what she calls transportation theory, or the way in which excellent long-form writing can 'transport' its reader into a 'carefully constructed narrative world' (p. 68). And she claims one of the keys to the notion of transporting readers is that even though it may not be enjoyable, empathetic connections are made to narrative content, be that people or events (p. 69).

In Chapter 5, Martin explains how the Virtue Map evolved through an earlier study she undertook into emotion in award-winning Walkley features. In that study, Martin applied her virtue mapping to 23 Walkley award-winning feature articles between 1988 and 2014. The Walkleys, the Australian equivalents of the US Pulitzer and the British Press Awards, are the premier journalistic prizes in the country. Chapter 6 is the final chapter of Section 1 and here Martin draws down on the meanings of emotion and its growing fascination within journalism studies, developing further the sixth element of her mapping phronesis, or 'the Master Virtue' (p. 126). She concludes this chapter with a thorough explanation and definition of the elements of her Virtue Map.

Section 2 presents her three case studies: Chapter 7 focuses on Helen Garner's 1993 feature 'Did Daniel have to die', written for *Time Australia Magazine*. Chapter 8 looks at 'The tall man', a long-form feature by Chloe Hooper, published by *The Monthly* in 2006 (and as a long-form book by Penguin Books Australia, in 2009); while in the third case study, Chapter 9, she analyses 'A betrayal', by Hannah Dreier, published in 2018 by ProPublica. All three texts are award-winning: Garner the 1993 Walkley for best feature; Hooper the 2006 Walkley for best feature, and Dreier the Pulitzer Prize for feature writing in 2019. In each case study, Martin carefully analyses sentence and phrase structuring to show how the three authors direct and observe for their audience; how they take us into the narrative spaces and places, and surround us with sensory renderings, creating that 'transportation' mentioned earlier.

In each case study analysis, Martin methodically italicises her six Virtue Map elemental words, proving how it can be operationalised to explain what it is that exemplary long-form writers manage with their craftwork in evoking emotions within their readers. Each case study has its own visual Virtual Map: Garner (p. 149), Hooper (p. 182) and Dreier (p. 216).

In the final Chapter 10, Martin brings home her over-arching impulse – to show how long-form writing can nourish a sense of community 'by performing the important cultural work of helping people live well together, to flourish' (p. 239). In her concluding words, Martin stresses how writers 'can use the alchemy of their words to move us to joy, to tears, to anger and even, most miraculously, to action, contributing to society's ongoing conversation it has with itself over how we can live a virtuous or "good" life' (p. 244). This book will make you think but, more importantly, in the hands of inspired educators, make the journalist of the future think, and truly consider her role in the industry of information gathering and dissemination. A must for every creative writing and journalism tertiary classroom.

Sue Joseph,
Associate Professor,
University of South Australia

Copyright 2023-1. Ethical Space: The International Journal of Communication Ethics. All rights reserved. Vol 20, No 1 2023 **87**

True biz

Sara Novic

Penguin Random House, 2022 pp 400

ISBN: 9780593241509

Through a blend of fiction and creative non-fiction Sara Novic has crafted an urgent and compelling lament of the demise of culturally important Deaf education In America. The fiction takes readers into the pleasures and pains of Deaf communities and outliers, whilst the non-fiction unwraps some mysteries of American sign language (ASL). The title refers to an ASL sign meaning real talk, or truth telling, and this is what Novic gives the reader.

Full disclosure here: I am Deaf, and this hearing loss complicates everything I do. I wish I had learnt sign language as a child, as a young adult even, instead of now, in middle age. My hearing parents made their decision for both their Deaf children that we would be 'normal' no matter what.

As Andrew Solomon explores in *Far from the tree* (2012), apples (Deaf children of hearing parents) are difficult fruit. I am one and got fitted with hearing aids and speech therapied into exhaustion. Teenaged Charlie, one of three central characters of *True biz*, is another difficult fruit and was cochlear-implanted as a young child. Her parents, like mine, were guided by medical professionals in the genuinely held but fallacious belief that oralism was the one true way to live, love and learn. Novic, a Deaf woman, relates how the cochlear implant enthusiasm in America meant that families who could afford the devices, the therapy and educational support had many children who did well; but families who couldn't afford these had failed implantees who were 'not cured' as the implant sales reps had promised. Those kids often wound up at Deaf schools, only now with vast cognitive 'defects' from childhoods with negligible language and minimal learning.

Charlie is isolated and friendless in a mainstream school with a dodgy dubious implant and no support. She is on the precipice of a fall into risky people, behaviours, drugs and crime. Thanks to a judge's ruling in her parents' divorce, Charlie is sent to River Valley School for the Deaf.

'True biz', as well as being a sign, is also a policy at this school where the headmistress, February, had introduced the policy 'as a way to get the students to talk to her when they were up to no good' and she would 'soften the consequences'. February noted so many of her students were failed by implants, hearing aids and therapies as children. Now, as these students navigated the complex language and fraught emotions of risk-laden teenage years, it's as if they were, in effect, 'a second wave of the terrible twos'.

After entering the endangered spaces of the residential River Valley School for Deaf and Deafblind children, Charlie begins to flourish. As her sign language blossoms, so too does her learning and social engagement with peers, parents and potential romantic partners. Charlie, with her newfound ASL skills, 'saw English, rigid and brittle, crack before her eyes – concepts that took up whole spoken phrases encapsulated in a single sign'.

Charlie learns that Deaf gossip is fast and virulent. She is befriended by Austin, a native signing teen and third main protagonist. He relates: 'If hearing people ever studied the power and speed of the Deaf rumour mill, they might think twice about classifying Deafness as a "communication disorder".'

Interspersed in a text that canvases multiple points of view, tricky ethical dilemmas and hazardous teenage behaviours is a curriculum of sorts. These non-fiction diversions are interleaved with the fictional text and are centred on the history of American Sign Language, evolution of Deaf culture, and activism. The headmistress, February, herself a CODA (child of Deaf adults), is teaching Charlie and the class about their place in the world, community and home.

There are two noxious undercurrents. Firstly, that society at large is audist, believing that hearing people are superior to people with hearing loss. In a hearing world, communication and care of Deaf people is parlous. Secondly, while the once floundering Charlie is blooming, the school itself is under threat of closure. February, notes sadly: 'The more vulnerable her student body was, the less politicians cared, or even pretended to care, about their fate.' The school is seeing the failed attempts at mainstreaming d/Deaf kids for they end up at specialist Deaf schools, but with 'vast cognitive defects'. Like a roll call for the fallen, *True biz* lists at the end, closures of (real) American schools for the Deaf in the past decades. One cannot help but wonder, where did all the Deaf kids go? And what happened when no one cared if and how they communicated, lived and learned?

Dr Annmaree Watharow,
Research Fellow,
University of Sydney

Speculative biography: Experiments, opportunities and provocations

Donna Lee Brien and Kiera Lindsey (eds)
Routledge, New York, 2021 pp 350
ISBN: 9780367515829

Speculative biography is a new foundational text for practitioners and readers of contemporary biographical writing. The book, edited by Brien and Lindsey, is comprised of four parts: the first is three contextualising chapters written by the editors, including an overview of speculative biography (by Brien and Lindsey), the place of speculative biography alongside history and fiction (by Brien), and an introduction to speculative biography and the narrative laboratory, which merges scientific methods of experimentation and evaluation with creative practice (by Lindsey). The ensuing three parts are named after the three titular designations: 'experiments', 'opportunities' and 'provocations'. The collective fifteen chapters focus on specific problems encountered during different stages of each author's writing and research processes. Each author works through the ethical, creative and methodological challenges that inevitably arise from work at the nexus of history and fiction. Each chapter is written in first person, highlighting the intrinsic self-reflexive nature of speculative biography.

If traditional biography crafts the life of an historical subject from available data and record, speculative biography goes further, delving deeper into the 'life world' of the subject, scouring the peripheries, engaging deeply with historical sources and, indeed, speculating about the gaps in historical knowledge to create more living, breathing characters with inner lives, dialogue and narratives of their own. Essentially, the speculative biography seeks to make a non-fiction text as compelling and engaging as a well-written novel.

As well as archive, artefacts and ethnographic source material such as interviews, the contributors experiment with environmental, animal, affective, cultural and even metaphysical sources in their speculative biographical work (p. 7). The chapter by Sarah Pye and Paul Williams 'Writing to save the sun bears: Speculating about non-human characters within biography' reflects on the ethical implications of inhabiting the inner life of a non-human subject, the critically endangered sun bear, as part of a biography of renowned Malaysian ecologist Dr Wong Siew Te. Pye writes: 'Ethically, my choice to include the subjective experience of sun bears in a non-fiction narrative needed to be based on the best science available, and what was known informed my speculation, but I felt it was important to indicate the gaps I was thus filling' (p. 122). The chapter provides an interesting discussion about the nature of biographical truth and inter-species connection, empathy and story.

    Copyright 2022-1. Ethical Space: The International Journal of Communication Ethics. All rights reserved. Vol 20, No 1 2023

Linda Wells, in her chapter 'Based on evidence and experience: The role of speculative biography in a decolonising reimagining of the Bungalow, Alice Springs 1914-1929' reflects on her project of writing a creative history of the Bungalow, a tin shed in Alice Springs referred to in official government documents as 'the Alice Springs Institute for Half-Castes'. In this work, Wells utilises techniques of speculative biography, fictocriticism, autoethnography and archival poetics in her creative non-fiction text. The chapter focuses on biographical subject Topsy Smith, who is the least represented in the archives, and through this case study discusses the central ethical consideration of decolonising research and writing practices. Wells reflects on processes of decolonisation through methods of enquiry (yarning, informal interview, ongoing collaboration with Indigenous people), intentions of language (not perpetuating historically offensive terms) and her broader place as a non-Indigenous researcher.

Paul Sandringham, in his chapter titled 'Speculative historical viability: A grave undertaking?' devises a prototype methodological framework for what he terms 'speculative historical viability' (p. 223) in the course of his work on a biography of forgotten politician Sir Isaac Isaacs (1855-1948). Sandringham is preoccupied by the historical viability of speculation, a common thread throughout the book: not only the speculation and re-creation of conversations and encounters, but subject motivations and connectedness of events, prompts the question: 'Does this [speculation] impair or enhance the historical usefulness and viability of my work?' (p. 224) Sandringham identifies the need for a new biographical approach to Sir Isaac Isaacs and highlights the key aspects of the biographer's self-perception and values which inform how he might conduct biographical speculations. Sandringham provides two case studies that demonstrate the tension between 'novelistic speculation and historical viability' (p. 229), inviting the reader to engage in the material and devise their own conclusions about Sandringham's argument.

Lindsey, in her chapter 'The speculative method', writes that stories, 'particularly the "true stories", which are the main business of the speculative biographer, are not only theorising activities in which we test evidence and synthesise analysis; they are also mysterious mediators of meaning which have the capacity to transform both hearts and minds' (p. 53). The provocations posed in the text are relevant to all writers exploring the space between history and fiction. A strong case is made for synergy between these traditionally opposing fields. Readers are compelled to reflect on the genre of biography, once reserved for the lives of heroic men, how far its conventions and traditions have been subverted and transformed, and speculate about the future of this increasingly robust and innovative genre.

Dr Tess Scholfield-Peters,
Researcher,
University of Technology Sydney

ethical
space
The International Journal
of Communication Ethics

Subscription information

Each volume contains four issues, published quarterly.

Annual Subscription (including postage)

Personal Subscription	Printed	Online
UK	£55	£25
Europe	£70	£25
RoW	£85	£25

Institutional Subscription	
UK	£185
Europe	£195
RoW	£210

Single Issue - Open Access £300

Enquiries regarding subscriptions and orders should be sent to:

Journals Fulfilment Department
Abramis Academic
ASK House
Northgate Avenue
Bury St Edmunds
Suffolk, IP32 6BB
UK

Tel: +44(0)1284 717884
Email: info@abramis.co.uk

Lightning Source UK Ltd.
Milton Keynes UK
UKHW051058190223
417246UK00007B/199